"And I sent messengers unto them, saying, I am doing a great work, so that I cannot come down: . . . " (Nehemiah 6:3).

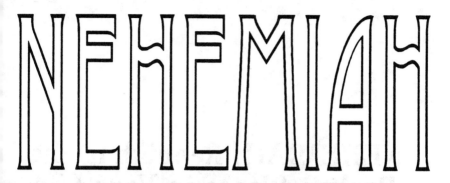

NEHEMIAH

Rebuilding the
Broken Places in
Your Life

BY MARILYN HICKEY

Marilyn
Hickey
Ministries

P.O. Box 17340
Denver, Colorado 80217

NEHEMIAH: Rebuilding the Broken Places in Your Life

Formerly titled: Your Personality Workout

Copyright © 1989 by Marilyn Hickey Ministries
P.O. Box 17340
Denver, CO 80217
All Rights Reserved

ISBN 1-56441-055-2

Printed in the U.S.A.

CONTENTS

CONTENTS

Chapter One

YOUR PERSONALITY CAN CHANGE

Everyone is very aware of his personality these days. We have available all kinds of classes on how we can change our personalities for the better, and—let's face it—some people really need the improvement. They're so impossible to be around!

We even meet some Christians who can really make us uptight. We comment, "He might be a Christian, but he doesn't act like one." Some people even say, "If that's a Christian, who wants to be one?"

Through the years as a pastor's wife, I have had really tough questions about how some Christians can be so difficult. Why do some people with seemingly beautiful, spiritual backgrounds have such ugly foregrounds? It seems that no matter what you say or do, they always have a negative reply. These types of people may just be difficult Christians, but God has a remedy for their personalities.

Even if your personality is good, God wants to finetune it and make it even better. None of us has arrived; we can all stand advancement toward a more Christlike personality!

This study will provide you with a way to rebuild any broken areas in your personality. Sometimes certain "walls" of our personalities have fallen to the ground, but it's good to know that they can be repaired by the knowledge of God's Word.

Proverbs 25:28 tells you, *"He that hath no rule over his own spirit is like a city that is broken down, and without walls."* Through this scripture God is saying, "A person who fails to control his personality is subject to attack." If the walls of a city are down, the enemy can come in. So our goal is to get the walls of our personalities rebuilt so that we can be fit temples in which God can dwell.

I found the most beautiful typology of how to rebuild damaged areas of our personalities in the little book of **Nehemiah.**

The book of Ezra is contemporary with Nehemiah. Ezra tells of how he was sent by God back to Jerusalem with a burden to help rebuild the temple. If you look into the historical background, you find that the Israelites had been in captivity for 70 years because of idolatry. It was a terrible time when they pined away for their God.

After the 70 years of captivity, which had been prophesied by Jeremiah, God told Israel, "Your time of punishment is over. You have been cleansed from idolatry, so I am going to let you return to rebuild your temple." Ezra was God's key man in the project, and the book of Ezra tells you how he was used by God.

With Ezra's help, the Israelites rebuilt their temple. When Jesus enters our hearts and lives, the Bible tells us that we have become temples of God:

> *"Know ye not that ye are the temple of God, and that the Spirit of God dwelleth in you?" (I Corinthians 3:16).*

When the Holy Spirit comes to dwell in our hearts by faith, God looks around and says, "This temple needs the protection of walls to keep the enemy out." So the book following the building of the temple is Nehemiah. It tells how God built up the walls surrounding the city of Jerusalem.

In Nehemiah you see a man sent by God to help make the temple safe from enemy onslaughts against Israel. The heart's desire of Nehemiah was to see the temple safe again. Because the walls had been broken down, the gates had crumbled. God put a tremendous burden on Nehemiah to mend the situation.

It is interesting that the meaning of Nehemiah's name is **Comforter.** Just as Nehemiah brought comfort to his people through the rebuilding and the promise of safety, the Holy Spirit is our Comforter who wants to rebuild our personalities. When He enters our hearts, He examines our personalities and begins a new process of restoration. The Comforter has come to strengthen our hearts, and He says, "I want to make you like Jesus."

You ask, "Does He really **enjoy** restoring my personality?" I know that He does, and I saw this in Matthew 18, a beautiful picture of a shepherd who made a great effort to restore one lost sheep to his large sheepfold.

A shepherd had a flock of 100 sheep, one of which wandered into the wilderness. Finding a sheep missing, the shepherd left his other 99 sheep in search of the one. The shepherd had to go far into the wilds, climbing over rocks, hills, brambles, and perhaps even falling several times. He probably crossed streambeds, and who knows what else. But when he finally found the lamb, his task had only begun. Then he had to return, carrying the sheep on his shoulders with its legs tied around his neck.

Did the shepherd consider the restoration of one sheep to the fold to be a drag and a drain? No way. In fact, the Bible says that he rejoiced, and when he brought the lamb home, all the neighbors rejoiced, too. God rejoices in restoring your personality.

You will find that Nehemiah was a "type" of the Holy

Spirit, and his complete strength and attention was focused on restoring Jerusalem's walls. Why was he so concerned about the walls of Jerusalem? The answer is found in the very first chapter:

> *But if ye turn unto me, and keep my commandments, and do them; though there were of you cast out unto the uttermost part of the heaven, yet will I gather them from thence, and will bring them unto the place that I have chosen to set my name there" (Nehemiah 1:9).*

God says, "Do you see this born-again Christian? I have set My name on him. He is a **Christ**ian now, and I love him because he bears my Son's name. Since that person bears My name, I don't want him to have a nasty disposition. I don't want him biting other people's heads off and being ugly. I want him to be like Me."

Then Nehemiah 1:10 tells you another reason that God wants to restore our personalities:

> *"Now these are thy servants and thy people, whom thou hast redeemed by thy great power, and by thy strong hand" (Nehemiah 1:10).*

The Hebrew word for **redeemed** means "to buy back." We sing hymns about being "redeemed by the blood of the Lamb," yet do we know what those words mean? We have been bought by God with the most expensive possession He owned: the blood of His only Son, Jesus Christ. "To buy back" says so much. When God bought us, we were **set free to do His will, freed from physical disease,** and **taken from prison and bondage into freedom.** God paid an expensive price to purchase these things for us; and if He bought us, He won't let us sit there like pieces of junk! He is going to restore us by conforming our personalities to His Son's perfect image.

In the second chapter you see Nehemiah venturing out toward Jerusalem. As soon as he arrives there, the enemy comes out—angry, upset and ready for violence.

One of the first things that happens to us when Jesus begins revealing some areas for restoration is that the enemy says, "Uh-oh." You can even see his thoughts:

"When Sanballat the Horonite, and Tobiah, the servant, the Ammonite, heard of it, it grieved them exceedingly that there was come a man to seek the welfare of the children of Israel" (Nehemiah 2:10).

It grieves the devil when he sees the Holy Spirit enter your life for the purpose of enhancing your well-being and bringing you life at its best. It upsets the devil, and you can especially see this when you know that the root meaning of **Sanballat** is "Satan."

You see, both God and the devil want to have control over your personality. What components make up your personality? Basically, this is where you think, feel, and choose. The walls in the book of Nehemiah represent your personality; but the gates are even more specific: they are the places of authority where you make decisions. God is very concerned about what choices you make in your life. He wants to lead you in making them by the direction of His Spirit.

To accomplish this, God has given you three main benefits for your personality. In your thinking, He has given you the mind of Christ. In your emotions, He has given you the ability to react supernaturally, and in your decisions He has given you spiritual leading by the Holy Spirit within.

Nehemiah wanted to build a strong wall, but when he came to Jerusalem there was quite a task ahead. The walls lay in piles of rubble. Nehemiah had been in Jerusalem for three days; when on the third day he arose, while the town slept, to have a closer look at the damage. Three, of course, is the number of resurrection. Nehemiah wanted to see what would be involved in resurrecting the ruins of Jerusalem's walls and gates.

Looking over the scene, Nehemiah saw rubble, rubble, rubble. There were broken and burned bricks, and debris lay everywhere. I thought, "The Holy Spirit wants to take the rubbish and debris from our past lives and sweep it out forever."

But in studying the book of Nehemiah, I discovered that it is not the Holy Spirit's plan to sweep away the broken bricks. His plan is to rebuild the walls, not build brand new ones. God is so economical; He takes your old, useless past life and uses it to create a productive present.

Through the years as a pastor's wife, I have been amazed to watch how God will save a young drug addict, fill him with the Spirit, deliver him from his addiction, and then send him right back to minister where he came from. The young person becomes a witness and an instrument to win former friends to Christ. His past becomes a strengthening force to help win people with similar pasts.

God can make your past a blessing, too. In Nehemiah the old debris was actually useful! So the Holy Spirit will use your past experience and turn it into something that glorifies God.

After seeing the rubble surrounding the walls, and the city gates hanging on rusted hinges, Nehemiah said to himself, "This must all be restored to its original condition." But Nehemiah was not planning to do the job alone; he would have the help of the whole city!

The Holy Spirit is not going to build your personality all by Himself. Of course, like Nehemiah, He directs the work that takes place. But just as Nehemiah called on the townspeople for help, the Holy Spirit will use other people in your life. That is His plan:

"Then said I unto them, Ye see the distress that we are in, how Jerusalem lieth waste, and the gates thereof are burned with fire: come, and let us build up the wall of Jerusalem, that we be no more a reproach" (Nehemiah 2:17).

Nehemiah said, "We are **all** involved in this project. Let **us** build." The Holy Spirit is present to direct the work in your soul and use your past; but He will also use people to help. God will place all kinds of personalities in your life to rebuild the walls and gates, and when I say "all kinds," I mean it! Sometimes He will use someone unexpected, because that person was the only one who could take care of a certain area of your life.

Studying all of the gates in Nehemiah (and you will see them in more detail), you find that all kinds of people helped hang the gates. There were goldsmiths (jewelers), apothecaries (druggists), daughters, noblemen, and Gibeonites. God does not say, "I'll just send really neat people with whom you have a great deal in common." He may send people you don't even like! He may even use unsaved people to help you.

It is very dangerous for us to close doors to certain people because "they aren't our type." I have been guilty of it. I have said, "God, we don't see eye-to-eye on things," and God has replied, "Don't close that door. I have sent that person to use him in your life."

13

Some years ago a woman in our church was really troublesome. She was very caustic and critical. Our church is called "Happy Church," so we should be happy, right? But that woman was bad advertising for us!

Once a year we held a business meeting, and one year when she attended the meeting, it wasn't a happy one. This woman stood up and said some really nasty things. She acted as though my husband and I were thugs, and she asked questions insinuating, "What are you **really** doing? Do the people **really** know what is happening?"

Her words cut me deeply. I must be honest that my attitude was very unspiritual. As the woman spoke, I turned around and gave a look that said, "Why don't you sit down and shut up?" Of course, she didn't look at me at all. She just went on asking questions.

The only person really damaged by that meeting was me. The rest of those present for the meeting knew the woman's attitudes were less than spiritual, so they ignored her actions. But on the way home my husband said, "Wasn't that a good business meeting?"

I answered, "No, I thought it was terrible."

He said, "You mean so-and-so? Oh, Marilyn, she is nothing to worry about." But the more I thought about the woman, the angrier I became. Soon I had become bitter.

The business meeting had been on a Wednesday night. The following Sunday morning as I greeted people after a church service, this woman raced over to me, grabbed and hugged me, and said, "Oh, I love you, sister."

I thought, "If that's love, forget it!" To be honest, I did not love her back at all. I didn't want her to tell me that she loved me, and I didn't say, "I love you, too." Instead I just kind of mumbled, "God bless you."

That day I went home with an ugly feeling inside toward that woman and did not realize that she would be used by God to rebuild a part of my personality that I desperately needed. Out of this experience I would receive a revelation from God that I had never seen.

During the day on Sunday I thought, "We are having communion tonight." The Bible says about communion that you can drink damnation to yourself if you take it while you have fought against your brother. I thought, "I don't want to drink damnation to myself." I began to pray and pray, "Oh, God, help me forgive her." The more I prayed, the less forgiving I felt! I became more and more upset with the woman.

At that time, our church's communion services were held differently than they are now. For communion, we dimmed the lights, and quietly sang and worshipped the Lord. Then people came and took communion as they felt spiritually prepared. Voluntarily, people would come to the altar, kneel and be served communion.

I thought, "I cannot take communion with this terrible unforgiveness. Nobody will know it anyway, because the lights will be down." The only person who might have known would have been my husband, Wally, because we usually took communion together. On the way to the church I told him, "I won't be taking communion tonight."

He almost fell out of the car!

He asked me why I wouldn't be taking communion and I explained, "I have unforgiveness in my heart." He said, "Oh, I just can't believe that." I thought his words were one of the sweetest compliments I'd ever received. He thought I couldn't feel unforgiving! I insisted, "It's true. I have un-forgiveness, and I can't get rid of it." Wally asked me to pray with him, and afterward he said, "Well, do you feel better?"

"No, I feel worse." We arrived at the church, held the service, and afterwards the lights were turned low for communion to begin. I sat alone, in a negative frame of mind, and then I found out that God is a tattle-tale. No one would have known that I had missed communion. But a woman from all the way across the church walked over to me and sat down. She said, "Marilyn, I feel led to take communion with you tonight."

I thought, "God, why did you do that?" Then I told the woman, "I won't be taking communion." She was almost as shocked as my husband had been! When she learned why, she nodded and said, "That's why the Lord sent me over here." She sat quietly for a few moments and then broke the silence, "Marilyn, you always tell us to take things by faith. Why can't you take forgiveness by faith?" When she said those words, it seemed that a light switched on and shone this scripture into my spirit:

"To whom ye forgive anything, I forgive also: for if I forgave anything, to whom I forgave it, for your sakes forgave I it in the person of Christ" (2 Corinthians 2:10).

I had been trying, trying, trying to forgive a sister all by myself. But I had not been forgiving her in the person of Jesus Christ. At that moment I prayed, "Oh, Jesus, I forgive her. I take forgiveness by faith and forgive her with your ability, not my own."

That prayer set my spirit free to worship. I took communion that night, and I will never forget that service. God had placed a brick in the wall of my personality about how to take forgiveness.

There is a sequel to this story. I never talked to the woman about my feelings toward her; but a month after the business meeting she called and said, "I know that you are very busy with services. Tell me how I can come over to your house and leave a meal in your refrigerator."

What happened? Afterward she called many more times and was always doing something sweet for my family. One day as I prayed, the Lord said, "When you loosed forgiveness in heaven, you loosed it on earth. You loosed that woman to do good works. But until you forgave her, heaven was bound from moving on earth to release her. The love you feel for that woman came through your forgiveness."

Then the Lord reminded me, "Remember the stoning of Stephen? He prayed, 'Lord, don't lay this sin to their charge.'" Stephen forgave Saul, who consented to the martyr's stoning. Later on Saul was loosed to become Paul, one of Christ's apostles and a writer of the New Testament. When Stephen loosed forgiveness for Saul, heaven came to earth in his life.

On his way to Damascus Saul fell to the ground under God's power, which came in a flash of blinding light. Saul cried out, "Lord? Who are you?" The Lord called him into ministry right then. Sometimes I think that God may have said, "Stephen didn't get to finish his work because you consented to his death. Now you get to finish it for him."

Can you see how God is using personalities to rebuild the walls and gates of our lives? When we close doors to people we dislike, or people who are different, or people who are impossible to get along with, we may be closing the gates to one whom the Holy Spirit has placed in our lives. God has a way for us to deal with those whom He sends to us, and we must not close our doors to them.

We say that some people are extroverts because they open all the gates of their personalities to let everyone in. Then we call others introverts because the gates of their personalities seem completely closed. Actually, both of these types of personalities need to be balanced as to how they deal with the people whom God sends. God wants us to know **when** to close the gates of our personality and **when** to open them. We are to have Spirit-led personalities that are being restored into the image of Jesus.

Would you say that the walls of your personality have been broken in certain areas? The Holy Spirit wants, right now, to begin rebuilding the walls and gates of your personality.

You may say, "Oh, but my past is terrible." But I looked at what God used to rebuild Jerusalem's walls, and He used burned bricks. Burned stones. It seemed very strange that He used burned materials, but then I began to see something special about them.

Today, when you go to buy stones or bricks for a building, the most expensive ones you can buy are those that have been used. The burned bricks make the most beautiful walls and fireplaces because they show a contrast. Not one is alike. God uses your past because there are certain people whom only you can reach.

The contrast comes in that you are a new creature in Christ Jesus. You are totally different from the person you were before being saved. People say, "I knew you before—but you have certainly changed!" They see the contrast that Jesus has made in your life, and it is beautiful. Then God uses that contrast as a witness and to help you rebuild the walls of other people's personalities.

We must be very keen to the Spirit's voice in helping other people, however. Sometimes I see older Christians approach new Christians and try to rebuild the walls without the Holy Spirit's help. The older, experienced Christian will say, "Stop smoking! You can't do this, and you can't do that!"

But when Nehemiah went out alone at night to examine the city's walls, he was very much in tune with the voice of God. He stopped first by a place called the "Valley Gate," which is a "type" of hell. This gate was where the city's garbage was burned.

Right beside the gate was a well called "Dragon's Well." I thought that was a strange name for a well, but tradition said, "A dragon was slain here." One of the devil's names is "the dragon." He was killed, so he can no longer drag you into hell.

Around the well there was a great deal of garbage and refuse. But Nehemiah didn't just rush in and start throwing everything away; he was waiting for the Lord to tell him his next move. In the same way, when we see garbage and trash in someone's life, particularly that of a young believer, we must be led of the Spirit in helping them. Otherwise, we can cause more harm than good.

I wondered why there was a pool by the gate, and I found that there was either a fountain, pool, or well by every gate in the wall. Why would there be water? The water was there to put out the enemy's fiery darts!

The gates in your personality are where you make decisions. The Holy Spirit may say, "Close the gate, here comes the enemy." But when you close the gate, the enemy may throw a fiery dart to catch the gate on fire. That's when you use water to put out the fire and keep your fortress intact.

The water represents the washing of the water by God's Word. How did Jesus put out fiery darts from the enemy? Jesus said, "It is written," and then spoke God's Word. You have to have the Word, as well as the Spirit, if your personality is going to reflect God's best for you.

How wonderful it is for us to experience the benefit of having a personality like that of Jesus! It's exciting to know that God wants to restore our personalities, day by day, in the power of the Holy Spirit. A transformed personality is God's high goal for us according to Philippians 2:13, *"For it is God which worketh in you both to will and to do of his good pleasure."*

Chapter Two

THE GATES OF AUTHORITY IN YOUR PERSONALITY

PART ONE

In the book of Nehemiah the gates represent places of authority in your personality. They are where you make decisions, whether "yes" or "no" to the enemy, and "yes" or "no" to God. Nehemiah tells of 12 gates, all but one of which are mentioned in the third chapter. The twelfth gate is found in chapter eight, and it is a very unusual gate. Let's identify each of the gates to find out how they were built and when they should be open or shut.

THE SHEEP GATE

Why would a Sheep Gate be mentioned first? The Sheep Gate was where animals were brought into the city for sacrifice. In our personalities this is where we first opened our hearts for Jesus to become our personal Savior. He is the Lamb of God who was sacrificed for sin in our places.

Without the Sheep Gate, there could be no restoration of our personalities.

Jesus is your personal lamb and your personal savior, but He is more than that. I traced the history of the sacrificed lamb to the Jews' departure from Egypt, when lambs were slaughtered on the doorsteps of all Jewish households. Afterwards these lambs' blood was traced over the doorposts. When the angel of death passed over Egypt that night, no death came to the households protected by the markings from the blood of lambs. Every family had a lamb, so Jesus is the lamb who was sacrificed for your loved ones, as well as for you!

Jesus is also the Lamb for nations. In Israel the priests sacrificed a lamb every morning and every evening for the sins of their nation. There was a tremendous concern that Israel, as a nation, would serve only the living God through daily atonement for any sin.

We say, "Is God just for the nation of Israel? Was He just for the Hebrew people?" No, God is for every nation. When John the Baptist saw Jesus in John 1:29 he said, *"Behold the Lamb of God, which taketh away the sin of the world."* Jesus is a Lamb for the salvation of the entire world. He is the one who makes it possible for believers of every nation to have personality restoration. He is the Lamb slain for you, your family, our nation and the world.

Many different types of people were involved in building and preparing the Sheep Gate. Nehemiah 3 says that both priests and laymen were involved. Eliashib, the high priest, helped hang this gate. His name means "God restores." How true. God restores through Jesus, the Lamb. Not just the leaders are responsible for hanging the Sheep Gate in the lives of unsaved people. You and I share that same responsibility of leading others to a relationship with the Lamb of God.

THE FISH GATE

The second gate that is mentioned in the third chapter of Nehemiah is called the Fish Gate. The word **fish** means "to wiggle." That word describes a new Christian, doesn't it? A new believer is so wiggly! He says, "If I had been saved for as long as everyone else, I would have converted the whole world!" A new Christian wants to do everything because he is so full of new life.

An infant is so full of wiggles and requires much work, but he is so delightful! Everyone is thrilled by each new development of a baby. With new Christians it is no different. Their enthusiasm is contagious. You see a new believer being baptized and it is very precious; or you watch him witnessing to all of his friends and growing in the Lord every day. I love new Christians, for they bring to a congregation that special freshness that can be brought by no other person. A new baby brings freshness to a home; so does a new Christian to the body of Christ.

Who built the Fish Gate? It is interesting that only a few priests helped. Most of the workers were everyday people. But Nehemiah 3:5 says, *"The nobles put not their necks to the work of the Lord."* Evidently the noblemen could not be bothered with new converts. Perhaps the ministries of these noblemen were "too deep." But I want to tell you, when a person's ministry is too deep for a new convert, that person has dug himself in too far. He will never dig out!

God wants the whole body of Christ to bless new Christians. We are all supposed to involve ourselves with the new ones. We are to love and encourage them and do as much as possible for them. Some people say, "That's a pastor's job." No, it is a job that was assigned by Jesus to everyone. Never think of yourself as too noble to help newly converted believers. Dedicate yourself to helping them grow in their walks with the Lord.

THE OLD GATE

Who wants an Old Gate? Most people want everything to be new! After all, aren't there enough burned materials in the walls without having an old gate, too? You need an Old Gate because there are some old things in your life that God wants to take out. He has a special gate through which bad parts of your past, such as hurts and fears, must come out. God wants to remove those things, and He has a gate especially for that purpose.

There are some things in your past that God wants you to use in helping other people. Sometimes you have received comfort, and God wants you to share that same comfort with another person. It is very important that we let God be in control of all the old things in our lives.

Who helped to hang the Old Gate? Many, many people from all walks of life were involved. There were goldsmiths (jewelers), apothecaries (druggists), rulers and daughters. Women helped to hang the Old Gate, as did a group of people called Gibeonites. I thought, "If anybody would know about taking out a bad past, it would be a Gibeonite!"

Perhaps you are not familiar with the Gibeonites, but they turned out to be some of my favorite people in the Bible. Initially they are found in the book of Joshua where they lived up to the meaning of their name, for the word **gibeon** means "a deceiver."

In Joshua chapter nine you find a group of Gibeonites telling Joshua and his princes, "We have traveled a great distance to this land." These people had long beards, old ragged clothes, moldy wineskins, and a very dirty appearance. They told Joshua, "We have heard about your mighty God. We heard that He killed your enemies Sihon and Og and parted the Red Sea. We have traveled a great distance so that we can make a covenant with you."

God had warned Joshua, "Don't make a covenant with any of the Canaanites." Since Joshua thought the Gibeonites were not from Canaan, Joshua agreed that a covenant could be established.

The problem was that the Gibeonites had not really traveled from a far country; in fact, they lived right there in Canaan! But they had heard the Word of God, feared it and believed it. They even went to the lengths of deception to be a part of it!

Joshua and his princes never prayed about the situation. They simply entered into a covenant with the Gibeonites: "We won't hurt each other. We will stand up for each other and even fight for each other." Everything was all set and ready to go because of the Gibeonites' deception of the Israelites.

If only Joshua had known the Gibeonites' history! Originally the Gibeonites were called "Hivites," and **hivite** means "snake." The book of Genesis tells us that Jacob had a daughter, Dinah, who was raped by a Hivite man named Shechem. Afterward he went home and told his father, "I want to marry Dinah."

Shechem's father told Jacob the whole story and then asked, "What must I do for my son to marry your daughter?" Jacob said, "All of the Hivites must accept

Jehovah God. Your men must all be circumcised."

The Hivites were willing to accept Jehovah God, so all of them were circumcised. But while they were still recovering, the sons of Jacob raced in and killed all of the men in revenge. Jacob was so upset and ashamed of his sons' behavior that he and his family had to leave the country. The sons of Jacob had deceived the Hivites, but bread cast on the water always returns. In the book of Joshua the sons of the Hivites now deceived the sons of Jacob!

Three days after the Israelites had made a covenant with the Gibeonites, Joshua discovered their deception. Three days is always the number of resurrection—Joshua and his men were resurrected all right; they had their eyes opened! The Israelites marched into Gibeon and said, "You lied to us!"

The Gibeonites admitted, "It's true, but we were afraid." Joshua was very disturbed. He consulted with his princes who said, "We cannot break a covenant. But we can punish the Gibeonites by making them serve in carrying water and wood to the tabernacle."

The Gibeonites became servants to the Israelites, and shortly afterward their covenant was put to a test. All of Canaan heard about the covenant between Gibeon and Israel. They said, "We are going to go down and fight against Gibeon." So the Gibeonites came to Joshua and asked for help.

Joshua prayed, "God, what should I do?" I'm glad that he prayed this time. He should have prayed the first time, and he wouldn't have been in this mess! God told Joshua, "Go out because you will win the battle."

As the Canaanites battled against Israel and Gibeon, the

night began to fall. Joshua knew that if darkness came too soon, Israel would lose the battle. He was such a man of faith that he said, "Sun, stand still. Moon, stay in the valley of Ajalon." God honored Joshua's words, the sky remained light, and Israel won the battle for the Gibeonites.

We say, "God, why did you win a battle for the people of Gibeon? They were liars and deceivers!" But God says, "They were new converts. I always have special miracles for new converts."

I would venture to say that the chapter about this battle is the greatest miracle chapter in the Old Testament, and it displays God's love for new converts to the faith. But this story has an even happier ending. The Gibeonites show up later in the book of Ezra as one of the first groups returning to build the temple in Jerusalem. But they are no longer called Gibeonites; they are called **Nethinims,** which means "devoted men of God."

No matter how bad the Gibeonites' past may have looked, God forgave them and brought them into victory. They knew that God forgave bad pasts. God also wants to take your past and make it a blessing because you are His devoted child.

THE VALLEY GATE

Nehemiah stopped at the Valley Gate on his third night in Jerusalem. This gate represents God's first miracle in your life—rescuing you from hell. He has rescued your personality, your body and your spirit from hell by building the Valley Gate in your life.

I looked to see who built the Valley Gate and discovered that a whole town of people were involved. God says, "Everyone is involved in taking people out of hell."

Everybody! The whole body of Christ should be praying, seeking God and asking Him to pour out His Spirit so that we can rescue others from the torment of hell.

I love to witness on airplanes and have always enjoyed personal soul winning. I remember one time my daughter and I prayed about a certain flight; we agreed that I would be able to witness to someone. I boarded my plane in a state of exhaustion and said, "Lord, You have to open this door. I'm surely not going to knock it down." Isn't that silly? After all, God always has to open the doors for us. We never knock doors down!

I exchanged a few casual words with the man sitting next to me and then out of the clear blue sky he said, "I just love to talk about religion." He really had my attention! I said, "I do too," and before that man reached his destination he had prayed and invited Jesus Christ into his heart.

The whole Body of Christ is involved in rescuing people from hell. Watch and pray for opportunities. Who knows, maybe today God will use you to help hang the Valley Gate in someone's life.

THE DUNG GATE

Everyone knows that dung is manure, but why would God have anything to do with it? God has a dung gate through which he removes the junk from your life. We must be sure to keep this gate open when God wants to remove something.

I looked to see who was involved in hanging the Dung Gate and found that a ruler hung the gate. Why would a man of authority fulfill this task? It is because God doesn't want us all dragging up garbage from other people's lives. When someone has fallen away from the truth the Bible says, *"You who are spiritual restore him"* (Galatians 6:1). God doesn't say, "Everybody restore him."

I appreciate the people in our church who stay away from the trash in other people's lives. Instead they go to a pastor and make him aware of any negative situations. They respect that correction should come from one who is in spiritual authority. When God wants to take garbage out of your life, open the gate of your heart. However, when others want to bring garbage into your life, keep the gate closed.

THE FOUNTAIN GATE

The Fountain Gate has a long, detailed description; I personally believe that this gate represents the baptism in the Holy Spirit. It delights me to think that God has a Fountain Gate to refresh the life of every believer.

Some people say, "We have the Holy Spirit at the new birth." But God doesn't want us just **having** the Holy Spirit; He wants us **overflowing** with the Holy Spirit! The Holy Spirit must have us.

Some believers close the Fountain Gate. They say, "I don't want to be baptized with the Holy Spirit." But every Christian needs to keep this gate open to God. After all, He put this gate in our personalities.

I looked at the description of the Fountain Gate and saw that a ruler set up the doors, locks and bars. Then there were many different people who were involved in its repair.

In the same way today you see people from every denomination receiving the baptism in the Holy Spirit. He is moving in the lives of Catholics, Methodists, Baptists and Lutherans, just to mention a few. You cannot limit the baptism in the Holy Spirit to the "holy roller" churches any more.

In Joel 2:28 God said, *"It shall come to pass afterward, that I will pour out my spirit upon all flesh."* That includes **you.** Don't close your personality to the Fountain Gate. It is one of the greatest helps that God has provided for your life.

A good friend of mine has always had a warm, wonderful and gracious personality; but before being baptized in the Holy Spirit, she had a hard time saying, "I'm sorry." But after she received the baptism in the Holy Spirit, her good personality became radiant!

Before I was baptized in the Holy Spirit I could never testify for the Lord. Once at a church service I was asked to share a testimony. The only thing I could say was, "I'm glad I'm here." When I sat down my husband-to-be nudged me and whispered, "You're a liar." It was true! I was not glad to be there because I did not enjoy fellowship with other Christians. The baptism in the Holy Spirit is what opened and transformed my personality.

When you feel attacked by personality problems, pray in the Spirit. You will find that your personality will then receive brand new strength as the power of the Holy Spirit flows through you.

THE PRISON GATE

Gate number six is called the Prison Gate and it symbolizes all the areas where we have been in bondage. Some of us have been imprisoned by habits, and others have been held captive to worry. But whatever the imprisonments are, God wants to free us from them.

We open the Prison Gate to remove wrong bondages, but then we must close it and imprison ourselves to God's will. God wants our wills bound to Him in faithfulness. He also wants us bound in faithfulness to the Body of Christ. It is in taking the identity of a bond servant that you will find your greatest freedom in Christ.

I discovered that the builder of the Prison Gate was a ruler. Why? It is because God does not want us running around telling everyone else how to be free. He wants to free us Himself. He is to be the ruler of our lives.

Chapter Three

THE GATES OF AUTHORITY IN YOUR PERSONALITY

PART TWO

It's exciting that God has placed gates in our personalities to indicate places of authority. These gates are where we make decisions—for God or for the enemy.

You have seen that there are fountains of water near the gates, so we can put out fiery darts with God's Word. Towers near all the gates symbolize where the Holy Spirit watches to help guide and direct your decisions of when to keep the gates of your personality open or closed.

So far you have seen the Sheep Gate, the Fish Gate, the Old Gate, the Valley Gate, the Dung Gate, the Fountain Gate and the Prison Gate. Your next gate is a very special one through which God brings His Word into our lives.

THE WATER GATE

In the book to Nehemiah the Water Gate was essential to

the Israelites, for through this gate came the city's water supply. The people couldn't just turn on a tap and have handy all the water they needed!

The builders of the Water Gate were Nethenims—you know who they were! They were the ancient Gibeonites, or Hivites, whose new name meant "devoted men of God." God brings devoted people into your life to carry His Word into your hearts, doesn't He?

When God brings people to carry His Word into your heart, don't close the gate, or you will shut out refreshment. Water refreshes you, and it also cleanses you. You can look into water and see the image of your face because water is like a mirror picturing back what you look like. In that way, God's Word shows you exactly where you stand with God and others.

The Water Gate must be open to God's Word, and not to false doctrine. Many times young Christians become concerned about whether they are receiving the right feeding. True, some are led into false doctrine, but I have noticed that the Holy Spirit is very protective of baby Christians to see that they receive the Living Word.

Years ago when we were holding church meetings in a store building, my husband and I were involved in an Oral Roberts city-wide campaign for Christ. As personal workers in the campaign, we received a list of new converts who were living in our area.

My husband personally called on those people and invited them to our church. We had just started a revival meeting, and four of the families that we invited came to that meeting. Remember, they were all brand new Christians who were probably only a week old in the Lord.

I was, of course, eager for the service to be just right for our visitors. Everything went well until the evangelist stood up to minister, and five men walked into the church and slammed the door behind them. They had everyone's attention—how could you help but notice them?

When the evangelist began to speak, the men were up-and-down, one after another, to go to the men's room. I thought, "Do they have kidney trouble, or what?" Then one man stood up in the middle of the teaching and began to prophesy. "In the name of Jeremiah!" He started running down an aisle, but the evangelist stopped him and said sharply, "We don't care to hear anything in the name of Jeremiah. We are here in the name of Jesus. Sit down, you are out of order."

We really had some spooks at that service! That night I was very upset about the situation. I told my husband, "Here were four families of brand new Christians who will probably never come back. They probably think we are a church of nuts, and I wouldn't blame them at all."

We prayed, and then we called on the families. As we drove to see them, the Lord sweetly assured me that He was working in all of these people's lives. He would protect them from being offended by the previous night's incident.

At the first family's home they were very excited about the Lord. The father said, "We really enjoyed the service last night, but then when the men stood up, we had the strangest feeling that something was wrong."

I thought, "These are the Lord's little babies. He is protecting them and causing them to discern the truth with the watchtower of His Holy Spirit." God is watching to see that baby Christians get the true Word! And the best part of the story is that we did not lose one family. God's Word can also be a discerner of truth in your life.

THE HORSE GATE

Why would you need a Horse Gate? In Jerusalem it was for carrying burdens in and out of the city. You know, God wants any wrong burdens out of your life. Cares are wrong burdens that He wants you to cast on Him. But at the same time, we are to help bear one another's burdens by praying for each other.

God will send to you Christians, to whom you must open your personality. Then God wants you to take their burdens to the Lord for them. But at times, we can become over-burdened. Sometimes we carry people's cares on ourselves without taking them to the Lord, and that isn't right.

The Horse Gate symbolizes that you should not become overburdened by either your own cares or the cares of others. You are also to minister actively to the Body of Christ by bearing their burdens in prayer. But you are to minister by being a vessel through which the Holy Spirit flows, not by taking everyone's cares upon yourself.

Sometimes people in the ministry feel overburdened because they hear problems, problems, problems all day. Unless they remember to take those burdens to the Lord, the load can become too heavy and cause the ministers to break.

Who was involved in building the Horse Gate? The priests were involved. Does that mean the laity doesn't have to bear any burdens? No, it doesn't, because the New Testament calls you a king **and** a priest in the Lord. You are called to minister as a priest in Him by praying for others. A priest is one who makes sacrifices, so you bring prayers and present them to God through the sacrificial blood of Jesus Christ.

The Lord saw that it was important for you to have a Horse Gate in your life. It is important that you use it to help bear people's burdens through the priesthood of prayer. This is essential to the completion of your personality. People who don't care about anyone getting saved, except their own families, are off the mark. God gave you a part of your personality so that you could carry burdens from other people's lives, as well as carry them from your own.

THE EAST GATE

The East Gate is the gate through which our Lord Jesus Christ will return to us in His second coming. It is believed that He passed through this gate on His way to Calvary. This gate in your heart is to create expectancy and hope as you look for the return of Jesus. When you lose contact with Jesus' promise to return, you lose comfort and strength. The Bible says that we find **comfort** knowing that Jesus is coming again for us (1 Thessalonians 4:18).

The East Gate is closely guarded by the Holy Spirit so that only the living Christ can enter it. No wonder Jesus warned, "Many will come in My name saying, 'Here is Christ.'" He wants the gate closed to anyone but Him.

Only one man built the East Gate, and he was the gate's keeper. Jesus said, *"Of that day and hour knoweth no man, no, not the angels of heaven, but my Father only"* (Matthew 24:36). Only the Father in Heaven, the keeper of the East Gate, knows when the Messiah will come back. But we have been told to live each day as though it were the day of Christ's blessed return.

THE MIPHKAD GATE

The eleventh gate found in Nehemiah chapter three is the

Miphkad gate, and **miphkad** means "assignment." God has a special assigned place for each of His people. He didn't say, "You're saved, so now just hang loose." He said, "I have designed a plan for your life."

Many people think this is predestination, but predestination means something different. Romans 8:29 says, *"Whom he [God] did foreknow, he also did predestinate to be conformed to the image of his Son."* You were not predestined to be saved or lost. That is not predestination, because 2 Peter 3:9 says that it isn't God's will that any person should perish. God, being omniscient, knows every person's decision; but He does not predestine your salvation or lack of salvation. Becoming a Christian is an individual decision. But God says, "My predestination for Christians is that they be conformed to the image of My Son." This is God's desire and plan for all believers.

God's assignment, or "miphkad," concerns your individual life. Don't think you're just an accident. God drew out a plan for your life in particular. What if you don't flow in that plan? Then you miss it, but you don't lose your salvation. Many Christians miss God's plan for their lives, but God still has that plan for them. We must be obedient to seek God's will so that we can flow in our assignments. Your assignment was meant to make you productive and a blessing to those whose lives cross yours.

You have to be sensitive and open toward God for His plan, because sometimes He calls you to do something that may seem distasteful. He may lead you into something where you tell Him, "This isn't my thing at all!"

Once when my husband and I were new in the ministry, we were invited to be assistant pastors in a large pentecostal church in Amarillo, Texas. I had heard that the church had a beautiful parsonage for the assistant pastors and I thought, "Wouldn't that be great?" Wasn't that a high spiritual motivation?

After we arrived to live in Amarillo, my husband and I were informed, "In all church history we have never done this, but we have hired two full-time assistant pastors. The other young couple is expecting a baby, and you don't have any children, so we are putting them in the parsonage."

The greatest blow to my life as a young wife had been when my doctors said, "You cannot have a baby," so the statement about our childless state stung deeply. Then I found that our new home was to be a tiny apartment that was also being called "home" by mice and cockroaches. It was grubby and dirty, so the pastor said, "I'll give you some paint."

Immediately I had **no** leading for us to stay in Amarillo as assistant pastors. I had no leading at all! This could not be God's Miphkad Gate for me, so I slammed it shut as hard as I could slam it. But my husband would not do the same. He said, "Marilyn, I told the Lord that I would go through any door He opened. I believe that He has opened this door, and I am going to go through it."

"And live here?"

"Yes."

"With the salary so low?"

"With the salary so low. This is God's place for us."

My husband helped me chase out mice and cockroaches, and we painted and cleaned the apartment. Amarillo was miserably hot, and the apartment was miserably small, so after a few weeks I told my husband, "I think you should resign."

He said, "No, the Lord has led us here."

I warned, "If you don't resign, I will leave." So I left Wally and went home to my mother. I told her, "It's too awful in Amarillo. I can't stay there." She was so sweet. She said nothing condemning, but I know that she prayed.

Then one day I opened my Bible to the book of Revelation, and a scripture practically jumped off the page, *"Behold, I have set an open door before you that no man can close"* (Rev. 3:8).

I quickly closed my Bible, but was nagged by the thought, "Have I closed the gate to God?" Yet God seemed to be saying, "I am holding it open, and you **will** walk through it."

I thought, "So I opened my Bible to a scripture. No big deal, it doesn't mean anything."

The next day an acquaintance of my mother's called and said, "The Lord has strongly impressed a scripture on my heart for Marilyn."

My mother told the woman, "You talk with her," and she handed me the telephone. The woman told me that she had a scripture for me, and I asked, "What is it?," dreading that it might be the same scripture in Revelation. And it was: *"Behold, I have set an open door before you that no man can close."*

I said, "Lord, I give up," packed my bags and went home to my husband and the church in Amarillo. You probably wonder, "How did it turn out?" It was one of the most delightful times of my life.

My husband and I worked hard, and we saw God move mightily in our lives. We held early morning prayer meetings and set up a visitation program. God opened a door for me to teach a class of young married people, and the class doubled, tripled and quadrupled. Marriages that had been broken up were wonderfully reconciled. I became very excited about the Bible because so much study was required in order to teach an adult class. Through that study I gained my first great desire to teach God's Word.

I had experienced difficulty accepting the Miphkad Gate that God opened for us in Amarillo; but when God opened the gate once again for us to leave, it was even more difficult. We had fallen in love with the assignment God had given us.

The Holy Spirit knows how to lead you in and how to lead you out. Look to Him and trust Him, and then you receive the best results in your life.

The Miphkad Gate was hung by goldsmiths (jewelers), and merchants were also involved. Even the Nethinims helped build this gate. Isn't that interesting? All kinds of people are used by God in causing you to flow in His divine plan. Have strangers ever been used by God to get you into God's plan? They have in my life.

Once I was flying to Buffalo, New York, and the plane I traveled on was prevented from landing in Buffalo due to a ground storm. I thought, "Oh no, I am going to be late to speak at the luncheon."

We had to land in Rochester, and I boarded the slowest bus that I have ever ridden. Midway to Buffalo the bus driver stopped to change for another driver. I was really beginning to feel panicky when the man seated across from me looked over and said, "Looks like you're going to miss your lunch today, doesn't it?"

I said, "It really does."

Then he said, "Well, they will be waiting when you get there."

When the man spoke those words, the Holy Spirit confirmed them, "That's right. They will be waiting." I arrived two hours late, and when I walked in where the luncheon would be held, the hostess came rushing over to me. She said, "You are just in time. The hotel mixed up our luncheon times! We were supposed to eat at 12:30, but they scheduled us for 1:30. We have **just** finished the last course."

I want to assure you that today God is using all kinds of personalities to cause you to flow with His will. It is His will that you flow in for a particular assignment that He designed. And in that assignment you find yourself being the most effective, fulfilled Christian you can be.

THE EPHRAIM GATE

The last gate is the Ephraim Gate, which is found in Nehemiah 8:16:

> *"So the people went forth, and brought them, and made themselves booths, every one upon the roof of his house, and in their courts, and in the courts of the house of God, and in the street of the water gate, and in the street of the gate of Ephraim" (Nehemiah 8:16).*

The Ephraim Gate is the "double-portion" gate. The Bible does not tell you who hangs this gate, but I think that the person responsible for hanging it is you. We may wonder, "Does God want me to have a double portion?" Oh, yes, He wants you to have a double portion. In the book of Deuteronomy you find that a double portion of inheritance was always given to the firstborn. Jesus is God's Firstborn, and we are His Body, so God has a double portion of inheritance for us.

You ask, "Why don't I have it?" James 4:2 says, *"Ye have not because ye ask not."* In Matthew chapter eight a centurion sought Jesus to heal his sick servant and said, *"I am not worthy that you should come to my house. Just speak the Word only, and my servant shall be healed."*

Jesus then marveled and said, "I have not seen faith this great in all Israel." Then He told the man, *"As you have believed, so shall it be done unto you."* You get that for which you believe! And the centurion's servant was healed in that very hour.

Double portion? God says, "You'll get it, if you believe Me for it." But nobody can hang your Ephraim gate for you. You have to hang it yourself by faith.

Chapter Four

OVERCOMING THE ENEMY OF YOUR PERSONALITY

You enter a battle zone when God starts building the gates and walls of your personality, and some of the battles seem impossible to win. You think, "I can't hang in there any longer! It's just getting worse all the time."

I want to show you some of the enemy's tricks; but even better—I want to look at how you can overcome them. You know, the devil hasn't changed; he isn't very original. You can see the same attacks on Nehemiah's building of the wall as you will see in the building of your personality. In Nehemiah chapter four the battle begins:

"But it came to pass, that when Sanballat heard that we builded the wall, he was wroth, and took great indignation and mocked the Jews. And he spake before his brethren and the army of Samaria, and said, What do these feeble Jews? will they fortify themselves? will they sacrifice? will they make an end in a day? will they revive the stones out of the heaps of the rubbish which are burned? Now Tobiah the

Ammonite was by him, and he said, Even that which they build, if a fox go up, he shall even break down their stone wall" (Nehemiah 4:1-3).

If you recall, Nehemiah's arrival in Jerusalem upset Sanballat terribly. Sanballat said, "Here is someone who cares about the welfare of the Israelites." The devil hates anyone who cares about God's people. He doesn't want you to live abundantly, and he certainly does not want your personality to be complete. The enemy hates and fears the work of the Holy Spirit in your personality.

Sanballat began to mock Nehemiah. He said, "Ha-ha. You think you're going to do something here? Forget it!" Then Sanballat's friend said, "There's nothing to that wall; a fox could knock it over." The enemy will tell you, "You can't change. Are you crazy? You've always been a failure."

I think that one of the most difficult persecutions is laughter. Sometimes ridicule is harder to take than outright verbal abuse! When someone scorns the Lord's work in your life, just remember that the devil isn't trying any new tricks. He wants to reverse the upward swing in your personality. Don't take it! Just say, "Satan, I am not ignorant of your devices, and I will not allow them to continue."

The Bible tells you exactly how Nehemiah handled every enemy attack. Nehemiah prayed,

"Hear, O our God; for we are despised: and turn their reproach upon their own head, and give them for a prey in the land of captivity: And cover not their iniquity, and let not their sin be blotted out from before thee: for they have provoked thee to anger before the builders. So built we the wall: and all the wall was joined together unto the half thereof: for the people had a mind to work" (Nehemiah 4:4-6).

Scorn and mockery from the enemy were overcome by prayer and people who had "a mind to work." They were all in agreement: "Let's get the job done." Sometimes we work hard but we don't pray. Other times we pray a lot, but we don't work. We have to overcome the enemy with both of these. When Satan comes with mocking words, just pray and keep on working.

The enemy's next device against Nehemiah was conspiracy:

> *"But it came to pass, that when Sanballat, and Tobiah, and the Arabians, and the Ammonites, and the Ashdodites, heard that the walls of Jerusalem were made up, and that the breaches began to be stopped, then they were very wroth. And conspired all of them to come and fight against Jerusalem and to hinder it" (Nehemiah 4:7,8).*

When "Plan A" failed, all the enemies gathered and put their heads together. They said, "We're mad! We're going to devise a secret plan to get those Israelites and stop them from working."

The devil has a plan to undo the work of God in your life. But you can overcome the conspiracies of the enemy:

> *"Nevertheless we made our prayer unto our God, and set a watch against them day and night, because of them" (Nehemiah 4:9).*

It is interesting to note how many times you find prayer in the book of Nehemiah. Prayer is a key weapon against the enemy's tactics because it gets your eyes off the problem and puts them on God. In Nehemiah 4:9 the people overcame conspiracy through prayer and preparation: *"Nevertheless we made our prayer unto our God and set a watch against them day and night, because of them" (Nehemiah 4:9).*

When enemies are conspiring against your plan the first thing you should do is hit your knees and pray. Be prepared a battle. Don't just hang loose, not read your Bible, panic and throw in the towel!

The Bible tells you, *"Having done all to stand, stand"* (Ephesians 6:13,14). But some of us have tried to stand without first doing all. We don't read the Bible, pray and fast, or prepare ourselves in any way for what is a spiritual battle. Don't be a lazy Christian. Prayer and preparation are essential for you to overcome conspiracy, anger and any other of the enemy's weapons including the next weapon used by Sanballat—threats.

> *"And Judah said, The strength of the bearers of burdens is decayed, and there is much rubbish; so that we are not able to build the wall. And our adversaries said, They shall not know, neither see, till we come in the midst among them, and slay them, and cause the work to cease. And it came to pass, that when the Jews which dealt by them came, they said unto us ten times, From all places whence ye shall return unto us they will be upon you"* (Nehemiah 4:10-12).

Sanballat and his friends said, "Go ahead and work. But we're going to drop into the midst of everyone and just start killing the workers." That's quite a threat. How do you handle threats, especially threats against your life? Let me tell you what the Israelites did, as is recorded in the lengthy passage of Nehemiah 4:13-23.

Certain workers were given swords, spears and bows and were assigned to protect the others who continued working on the wall. Some fortified the wall while others built. Day and night they were on guard against the enemy.

In the Body of Christ it takes some to pray, fast and hang in there to watch over those who are out actively ministering. I know that it has given me great strength to have certain people say, "Marilyn, I really prayed and fasted for you during that time."

Once God opened a door for me to appear on the Tom Snyder Show, a midnight program that was aired nationally on NBC. The program was to feature women who were evangelists. From watching the host I gathered that he could really knock people down with his words. He just zeroed in on them and undid them in a very critical way. I thought, "What might he say to three women who are in full-time ministry?"

A whole group of people from my church set aside the day on which we taped the show, and they fasted and prayed all day. That night they also came together and prayed. And do you know that the first question Tom Snyder asked was, "Can you tell me how to be born again?"

For one solid hour that program starred the Lord Jesus Christ. For one hour no one was exalted but Jesus. Then at the end Tom said, "You know, I'd like to host programs like this four nights out of five each week. This was so much fun." Then he invited us to come back.

How did that wonderful experience come about? It came because people were prepared with the weapons of spiritual warfare. They said, "We're building a wall for Jesus, and the devil cannot touch it." It takes constant preparation if you want to see your personality to mature into the fullness of Jesus Christ.

A certain woman in our church turned against my husband and me one time, and I felt very wounded. I wanted to call the woman and tell her off. Then I prayed, "Lord don't let me react with my reactions. Let me react with Yours." In the end I discovered that the woman was not really upset with my husband and me. Because she had been under tremendous pressure at home, she had taken it out on us. Instead of allowing me to tell her off, the Lord had led me to minister to this woman and encourage her in faith.

When threats and wounds come along, God has placed the Body of Christ around us for fortification so that we might win over our trials. The walls of your personality will be built and the gates will be hung. The enemy cannot win, because Jesus is going to see that your personality is conformed to His.

Nehemiah and his people handled problems from the outside beautifully! But as soon as the last attack ended, an even worse one came along. Eventually disunity broke out among the ranks. Can you imagine having to deal with quarrels after having been through those last attacks? They were too busy to waste time fighting with one another!

The people who worked on the walls discovered that creditors who had lent them money were charging exorbitant interest rates. Because of working on the wall, those in debt could not pay their bills. Therefore, they were losing property and everything they owned to their creditors.

As soon as Nehemiah heard about this oppression of the debtors he said, "This fighting isn't going to help anything!" Then he put an end to disunity by admonishing his people. To **admonish** does not mean "to rebuke." It means "to teach and train." I love the way Nehemiah didn't just thump people's heads and scream, "You're wrong!" He said, "This is wrong, but let me show you God's way." He had to explain to the creditors the damage of mistreating their fellow men.

The devil will rebuke you. He will throw you on the ground

and condemn you! But God will convict you and then give you a solution with which you can overcome the problem.

Instead of allowing disunity to break up the ranks, Nehemiah admonished them so that they could repent and come through in greater strength. Colossians 3:16 says, *"Let the word of Christ dwell in you richly, in all wisdom; teaching and admonishing one another."* It is interesting that it says, "Before you admonish, the Word of God has to dwell in you richly."

This is the ministry of helping our brothers to mature, for **admonish** really means "to mature." It is a word full of hope. It is a word of putting people over, not under:

> *"And we beseech you, brethren, to know them which labour among you, and are over you in the Lord, and admonish you; And to esteem them very highly in love for their work's sake. And be at peace among yourselves. Now we exhort you also brethren, warn them that are unruly, comfort the feebleminded, support the weak, be patient toward all men" (1 Thessalonians 5:12-14).*

God wants personalities in your life to help you overcome, not fail. He never sends people to rebuke you and put you down. Often you can perceive that the enemy is using someone simply because he condemns, rather than convicts. I'm not saying that someone cannot point out a weak area to correct it. But he is not supposed to leave you dangling in defeat. The person who says, "Admit it, you've never done well," is dropping a package of hopelessness at your feet. That is not the voice of God; that is the voice of Sanballat.

Nehemiah overcame disharmony by lifting the people up out of the mess. But it was at this point in the story that the enemy began to get really crafty:

"Now it came to pass, when Sanballat, and Tobiah, and Geshem the Arabian, and the rest of our enemies, heard that I had builded the wall, and that there was no breach left therein; (though at that time I had not set up the doors upon the gates;) That Sanballat and Geshem sent unto me, saying, Come, let us meet together in someone of the villages in the plain of Ono. But they thought to do me mischief" (Nehemiah 6:1,2).

Nehemiah received a message from his enemies that said, "Let's sit down and have a little friendly talk to straighten out the situation." But Nehemiah discerned their true purpose in writing to him, and here is how he answered:

*"I sent messengers to them, saying, I am doing a great work, so that I cannot come down: why should the work cease, whilst I leave it, and come down to you? Yet they sent unto me **four times** after this sort; and I answered them after the same manner"* (Nehemiah 6:3,4).

Nehemiah received messages not once, but four times! And he said, "I answered the same way each time." You see, he overcame the devil's craftiness with wisdom and work. The devil wants to get you to quit. He'll say, "Stop working and get involved in a fight." Then you won't be out doing the Lord's work. When the devil tries to sidetrack you, don't even answer him. Don't give him the time of day. Just keep right on working and you won't be embroiled in a lot of garbage.

The enemy's next trick was treachery. Sanballat sent a message to Nehemiah saying, "There is a prophet here who is prophesying against you." But the Lord helped Nehemiah to perceive the truth, and he did not listen to the false prophecy:

"And I said, Should such a man as I flee? and who is there, that, being as I am, would go into the temple to save his life? I will not go in. And, lo, I perceived that God had not sent him; but that he pronounced this prophecy against me: for Tobiah and Sanballat had hired him. Therefore was he hired, that I should be afraid, and do so, and sin, and that they might have matter for an evil report, that they might reproach me" (Nehemiah 6:11-13).

The Holy Spirit will give you discernment when the enemy comes against you with words of fear. That's why we need to be led by the Spirit. Treachery was overcome by the discernment of God's voice.

The enemy came with scorn and mockery, conspiracy, anger, threats and disunity. He came with craftiness, accusations and treachery. But Nehemiah never did stop working and say, "It's just too much. I give up." In every instance the Holy Spirit caused Nehemiah to overcome the enemy. The Holy Spirit wants to make you an overcomer too. Greater is He that is in you than he that is in the world. God does not want your personality in a mess. He does not want you to be hard to get along with and difficult. He wants you to be an overcomer! He that is in you will overcome the forces of evil around you. Nehemiah won the victory, and it had quite an effect on the enemy:

"And it came to pass, that when all our enemies heard thereof, and all the heathen that were about us saw these things, they were much cast down in their own eyes: for they perceived that this work was wrought of our God" (Nehemiah 6:16).

They knew that Nehemiah was doing God's work! How did they know? Because Nehemiah exercised prayer, self-control, bravery and strength to fulfill his calling. All of those qualities were given to him by God, and God wants to pour those same qualities into you.

I want you to know that the enemy has already been overcome. His deeds were put down when Jesus went to the cross and then rose from the dead. The enemy's fate has been sealed and settled, and all you have to do is appropriate the victory that you have in Jesus. Today Jesus wants you to enter into His victory and put down the enemy's works as you start becoming the complete personality that was assigned to you at the new birth.

Chapter Five

GOD'S REMEDY FOR AN INFERIORITY COMPLEX

One of the greatest needs in our lives today is the need to be free from an inferiority complex. All of us have areas in our lives where we feel inferior to other people. I heard a joke about a man who said, "I had an inferiority complex until I found out that I really was inferior." Actually, that joke loses its humor when you stop to think that too many people think they are inferior. Inferiority is one of the worst feelings a person can have!

I want you to look at a Biblical example of a man who had one of the worst inferiority complexes I've ever seen. But God took this man, step by step, out of inferiority into achievement. God had to use this man to bring the nation of Israel out of a state of deep trouble that had come because of their refusal to serve God. In order for God to use this man as a deliverer, first he had to be delivered from the complex of inferiority on his life.

God had warned the Israelites that if they served idols, the Canaanites and neighboring heathen tribes would become like "thorns" in Israel's side. God had said, "If you serve idols, you'll regret it," and Israel was regretting their idolatry because of the people of Midian.

The Midianites were a nation of cruel, abusive people whom God allowed to come against Israel. The people of Israel were so frightened that they were digging holes in the ground to live in, or living in caves, just to escape the Midianites.

Finally the Israelites cried out, "God, help us!" Any person who cries out to God for help is going to receive help, but the Israelites' aid did not come exactly as they had planned. They thought that God was immediately going to send them a mighty deliverer. But God didn't send a deliverer at all, in the beginning. He sent a prophet who came in and rebuked the people for their sin.

The prophet told the people of Israel, "Until you correct your relationship with God, forget about changing the problems in your relationships with others. God led you out of Egypt with a mighty hand, and what have you done? You turned to serve the god of the Amorites, in whose land you dwell. You need to repent!"

Then God told His people, "I am going to send you a deliverer." He had already chosen a man who would deliver the nation of Israel from the Midianites. His name was Gideon.

From appearances, Gideon had everything going for him. His name means "tree feller," or "muscle man," so he might have been a Mr. America in our day. He was the son of a man named Joash, and God called Gideon's family "outstanding" in the book of Joshua. You might say, "Gideon had what it took to be a leader!" But even with all of his positive attributes, Gideon had a serious inferiority complex.

When God sent an angel to Gideon, he was hiding from the Midianites. You can imagine his shock when, in the middle of such a desperate time, the angel spoke these encouraging words:

"The Lord is with thee, thou mighty man of valor"
(Judges 6:12b).

Gideon looked up and said, "Oh, really? Well, if the Lord is with us, why are the Midianites destroying Isreal? Where are the miracles our fathers told us about? Where is God?"

God did not reprove Gideon for his complex. God didn't say, "Gideon, aren't you listening to Me?" Instead, God gave Gideon another positive scripture:

"And the Lord looked upon him, and said, Go in this
thy might, and thou shalt save Israel from the hand of
the Midianites: have I not sent thee?" (Judges 6:14).

God was saying to Gideon, "If I am sending you, you won't fail. Don't worry about failure, Gideon." That's really positive. You see, Jesus did not intend for us to be inferior. He wants us to be superior. When the Lord sat down at the right hand of the Father, His work was finished. He had defeated the devil, hell, sin, the flesh, the world, and we are now seated in heavenly places with Him. God says, "If I'm with you, you'll have victory."

Then Gideon told God, "How can I save Israel? My family is poor in Manasseh, and I am the least in my father's house." Don't believe that statement, because it is a lie. You already know that Gideon's father was a town leader, and that his family was called "outstanding." Not only that, but Gideon himself had ten servants. How many of us have ten servants? Yet God wasn't choosing Gideon as a deliverer because of his status. Gideon, in spite of his inferiority complex, had a soft heart toward God. And God just kept giving Gideon more positive scriptures:

"And the Lord said unto him, Surely I will be with thee, and thou shalt smite the Midianites as one man" (Judges 6:16).

The best way to get someone out of a negative complex is to start telling him what God's Word says: "He that is in you is greater than he that is in the world." "Be of good cheer, you have overcome the world in Christ." God just tells you who He is, and reminds you that He is with you.

Gideon told the angel, "Since I have found grace in your sight, give me a sign that you have talked with me. Don't leave until I have made a sacrifice." Gideon brought a kid goat, along with some other things, and arranged them according to the angel's instruction. When it was ready, a fire came up out of the rock and consumed the sacrifice. God wanted Gideon to have a miracle to see that God was personally interested.

Sometimes we just need to see a miracle, don't we? I know of several times that God has allowed me to have miracles. He has made me use my own faith when I have felt chicken-hearted. For instance, once after a church service on Sunday night, I came home feeling sick, sick, sick. I felt exhausted, and my stomach was uneasy.

The next morning I had prayer, but that night I began feeling sick again. I started coughing, so my friends started praying some more. The next day I felt no better, but I knew that I needed a miracle soon. I had to be in Houston in two days, so I needed a miracle of healing. The next morning I felt sicker than ever. I was unable to get out of bed and was stumbling around from weakness when I tried to walk.

I couldn't go to Houston, I couldn't leave my bed—I didn't even want to talk to anyone. I was still depending on my friends to have faith for my healing. Then the Lord began dealing with me, "I want you to have faith for yourself."

"I'm too sick. I don't even feel like praying. I want other people to believe for me." At that point I was so hot that I took my temperature, which was 103°. I thought, "I hope someone is praying, because I am really sick." Then the Lord said, "What is wrong with your faith, Marilyn?"

"I don't have faith, Lord."

He said, "You do have faith." I looked at my thermometer again and rebuked the high fever. I said, "In 30 minutes I need to have a radical drop in my temperature. I demand it in Jesus' name." In 10 minutes' time the fever had dropped to 102°. In 20 minutes it was 101°, and in 30 minutes it had dropped to 100°! In the next hour my husband came home, my temperature had become normal, and I was hungry again.

The next day I went to Houston as planned. The Lord's powerful miracle of healing was such a personal statement of victory for me. It showed me how positive God is about wanting me to have faith, and it helped build my faith for future victories.

When Gideon saw the miracle of the fire consuming his sacrifice, he said, "I have seen God! I am going to die." Then the Lord spoke to Gideon, "Peace be unto you." Did you know that Jesus wants you to have peace? He said, *"Peace I leave with you, my peace I give unto you: not as the world giveth, give I unto you. Let not your heart be troubled, neither let it be afraid"* (John 14:27). Whatever God is doing in your life, He says, "Quit worrying! Take My peace."

Peace comes to you in Jesus. Peace doesn't just mean that

you aren't fighting with someone; it means that you are living life at its highest. God was giving Gideon peace—the knowledge of life at its best—even before the battle started!

That day Gideon saw God revealed as **Jehovah Shalom,** meaning, "Jehovah revealed peace to me." Don't you think that was a beautiful day?

Look at how God brought Gideon out of an inferiority complex. God quoted positive scripture about Who He is, He gave a visible miracle, and He gave Gideon peace.

After God did these things, you find that Gideon stopped asking so many questions and became much more cooperative. Still, God didn't lead Gideon out immediately into battle. Just as Gideon was led, step by step, out of an inferiority complex, he was being led by God, step by step, into victory.

> *"And it came to pass the same night, that the Lord said unto Him, Take thy father's young bullock, even the second bullock of seven years old, and throw down the altar of Baal that thy father hath, and cut down the grove that is by it" (Judges 6:25).*

Gideon gathered his servants to help him carry out God's instructions. They did this at night because, frankly, Gideon didn't have the guts to do it by day. But he didn't need to worry about being found out, because God happens to be a tattle-tale, and God told on Gideon.

The next day the men of Gideon's city arose early to go to their altar of Baal, but the altar was gone, and the grove had been cut down. Instead of seeing an altar to Baal, the men saw an altar to Jehovah God upon which a bullock had been sacrificed. Then the men began to ask, "Who did this?" Another man spoke up, "It was Gideon, the son of Joash."

God didn't let Gideon off the hook. He was found out anyway.

The men said, "Gideon has insulted Baal, so we have to kill him." At this point in the story, Gideon suddenly became fired up. He became the "muscle man" that his name indicated and said, "Come on! Isn't Baal big enough to fight his own battles? If Baal is mad at me, let him fight and kill me?"

The men who worshipped Baal thought, "That's fair enough." They named Gideon "Jerubbaal," which means "Baal is going to get you." These names are so important in helping us understand the full meaning of what happened. Later in 2 Samuel 11:21, Gideon is called "Jerubbasheth," which means "God has put to shame." Since Baal never did take revenge on Gideon, God put Baal to shame.

After Baal's followers had renamed Gideon, the Midianites arrived in town. But they didn't come alone; they brought the Amalekites with them. Can you imagine Gideon's looking on and wondering, "God, where are you?" But God was ready to help Gideon face his enemies, so the next thing He did was make Gideon a charismatic!

"But the spirit of the Lord came upon Gideon, and he blew a trumpet; and Abiezer was gathered after him" (Judges 6:34).

This is very interesting in the Hebrew translation. The words "came upon," basically mean that Gideon was clothed from his head to his toes in the Spirit of God. Isn't that great? Gideon's personality may have been full of holes, but God took care of those holes by clothing Gideon in the Spirit. But even after the Spirit came upon Gideon, he still had some problems with reverting back to his old inferiority complex.

Soon he began thinking, "I wonder if this is really God calling me?"

You may think, "This is quite a problem with Gideon!" But God wants to show us the worst case to prove that He can cure all of us from inferiority.

Wanting to be sure about the Lord's call, Gideon said, "I am going to lay a fleece outside on the ground. In the morning, if the fleece is wet, but the ground around it is dry, I'll know that this is God." God answered Gideon's fleece. Then Gideon said, "God, don't be mad, but I want to make sure one more time. This time let the fleece be dry and the ground all wet."

God answered Gideon's fleece again. I thought, "Oh, God, you are so patient." God is very patient to help people who have inferiority complexes. He wants so much to build a sense of assuredness and security in them.

Once in dealing with my son, I learned something about people with inferiority complexes. It proved how careful we must be to not build inferiority complexes in others. I asked my son, "Haven't you finished mowing the lawn yet?"

He said, "No, I'm just lazy."

I told him, "Don't ever say that about yourself! That is a terrible thing to say."

"Well, you say it."

I never again said that my son was lazy. We need to build patiently and not destroy, just as God patiently built confidence in Gideon's life.

At the same time that God was building, everybody else was calling Gideon, "Jerubbaal," or "Baal is going to get you." Imagine everybody calling you that, rather than your real name. How could you feel better about yourself? But

Gideon felt even worse when he woke up the next morning and found that Israel had been infiltrated by Midianites and Amalekites.

When Gideon found out that the enemies had come in, he rallied the people together, and 32,000 people showed up. That sounds like enough people to do the job, doesn't it? But then God told Gideon, "These are just too many people. If all these people win the battle, they will take the credit instead of giving it to Me. Send every fearful person home."

God's advice was, of course, very scriptural because the book of Deuteronomy says that if a man had just taken a wife, planted a crop, or was afraid, he could go home from battle. Gideon said, "Everyone who is afraid can go home," and 22,000 of the people left. Gideon wasn't the only one with an inferiority complex, was he?

Gideon was probably wondering, "How will we fight a battle with only 10,000 people?" But God spoke up, "These are still too many people."

"What are you trying to do, God? Kill me?"

God said, "Lead the people to the water and let them drink. Those who put their whole faces in the water to drink have to go home, but those who cup the water in their hand will stay for the battle."

Gideon brought the people to the water, and 9,700 of the men put their faces in the water to drink. Now Gideon had 300 men. By this time Gideon may have been thinking of surrender. But that night as he prepared to take his rest before the battle, God said, "Gideon, if you are still afraid, I want you to do something else."

What do you mean, "If Gideon is still afraid?" Of course, he was afraid, knowing that he and only 300 men would face the Midianites **and** the Amalekites! God said, "Take your servant and go listen to the Medianites as they are talking in their camp."

Gideon and his servant sneaked down to the Midianite tents, and as they approached the camp, they heard two men talking. Here is the conversation that Gideon overheard:

"Behold, I dreamed a dream, and, lo, a cake of barley bread tumbled into the host of Midian, and came unto a tent, and smote it that it fell and over-turned it, that the tent lay along. And his fellow answered and said, This is nothing else save the sword of Gideon the son of Joash, a man of Israel: for into his hand hath God delivered Midian, and all the host" (Judges 7:13,14).

Who caused the Midianite man to dream this dream? It was God, the tattle-tale! Isn't it strange that the man dreamed of a barley loaf? God was saying to Gideon, "You and your men are far more than just a little piece of bread or a few crumbs. You are a whole barley loaf! Some people might think you're an oaf, but you're a loaf!"

The man's confession of his dream deeply touched Gideon, and the Bible tells us that upon hearing the interpretation, Gideon "worshipped the Lord." Gideon returned to the Israelite army and said, *"Arise, for the Lord hath delivered unto your hand the host of Midian"* (Judges 7:15b).

The men of Israel were divided into three companies, and every man had a trumpet and an empty pitcher with a lamp in it. Gideon said, "When we come to the outside of the enemy camp, do exactly what I do. When I blow my trumpet, I want you to blow your trumpets and shout, 'The sword of the Lord, and of Gideon!'"

I thought, "Gideon, you aren't the timid little thing you used to be. You're even putting your name in there!" Gideon knew who he was, because God had healed him from an inferiority complex. Step by step, Gideon was delivered and shown his ability in God.

After reaching the Midianite camp, all the men followed Gideon's actions, blowing their trumpets and shouting, "The sword of the Lord, and of Gideon!" Then each man struck his pitcher, and when the pitchers broke, the lamps were struck by the cold night air, and each one lit up.

Aren't we the same way? The Bible calls us, "earthen vessels," and it calls God's Word a "two-edged sword that divides soul from spirit." When God's Word hits our earthen vessels, it creates more than a hairline crack. It breaks us so that Jesus' light can come shining through.

The Israelites' light began to shine, and confusion broke out in the ranks of the Midianites. Can't you imagine their confusion when, all of a sudden, they heard hundreds of trumpets, pitchers shattering, and men shouting, and saw light shining all around? Instead of running for help from the Amalekites, the Midianites began fighting with the Amalekites, and they began killing each other off!

The Israelites then chased after the Midianites and Amalekites, and as they did so, they called for additional men to fortify the ranks. Gideon called the men from the tribe of Ephraim, "Come down quickly!" The men from the tribes of Ephraim, Nephtali, Manasseh and Asher all came to help, and they all started killing Midianites right and left.

In this part of the battle the tribe of Ephraim is especially recognizedfor slaying two Midianite princes, Oreb and Zeeb. But these victories don't end the story. In the end you see Gideon as a different man than the easily intimidated man he had been when he was first called by God.

In Judges chapter eight the men of Ephraim asked Gideon, "Why didn't you call us to fight in the beginning?"

If I had been Gideon, my natural response would have been, "Look, guys, I called 32,000 men from my own tribe, but 22,000 of them went home because they were afraid. Then God told me to send home everyone who lapped the water like a dog, and that was another 9,700 of them. I only had 300 men to fight! If you don't like the way I handled it, talk to God. He's the one who gave me directions."

We can really be defensive—especially with relatives. Ephraim had been Manasseh's brother, so both tribes were originally sons of Jacob. Nobody can get under your skin more effectively than a relative—but the men of Ephraim didn't bother Gideon at all! In fact, he had a beautiful reaction:

"And he said unto them, what have I done now in comparison of you? Is not the gleaning of the grapes of Ephraim better than the vintage of Abiezer? God hath delivered unto your hands the princes of Midian, Oreb and Zeeb: and what was I able to do in comparison of you? Then their anger was abated toward him, when he had said that" (Judges 8:2,3).

First Gideon esteemed the tribe of Ephraim above his own tribe. And in his comparison Gideon didn't even mention his own name, but instead he spoke of Abiezer, his grandfather. Then Gideon said, "You're far better than I am, because you killed the princes of Midian! Nothing I've done compares to that." Gideon had become so secure about his ability in God that he didn't have to be defensive. It was more important to him to keep peace with his brothers.

66

Years later Solomon in his wisdom wrote, *"A soft answer turneth away wrath"* (Prob. 15:1). In the example of Gideon his soft answer and unwillingness to quarrel turned away the anger and contention of the men of Ephraim. I see in Gideon a truly Spirit-led, Spirit-filled personality. But it took God's dealing for Gideon to reach that place of security.

How was he delivered by God from an inferiority complex? God lifted him with the Word, filled him with His Holy Spirit, showed him several miracles, gave him peace, and brought victory. That is exciting. But even more exciting, if you will look to God for these same things, He will do for you what He did for Gideon.

Chapter Six

DEDICATING YOUR PERSONALITY TO GOD

God wants us to have complete personalities, but then He also wants our personalities to be dedicated to Him. The twelfth chapter of Nehemiah shows all of God's people gathering together to dedicate the walls and gates to Him. It wasn't just a few people coming together for a small dedication. Singers, musicians, princes, farmers and merchants from all over the land came to dedicate the walls to God.

Then you find that the dedication was not a dry, dull occasion, but it brought the people great joy:

"And at the dedication of the wall of Jerusalem they brought the Levites out of all their places, to bring them to Jerusalem, to keep the dedication with gladness, both with thanksgivings, and with singing, with cymbals, psalteries, and with harps" (Nehemiah 12:27).

"Also that day they offered great sacrifices, and rejoiced: for God had made them rejoice with great joy: the wives also and the children rejoiced: so that the joy of Jerusalem was heard even afar off" (Nehemiah 12:43).

When you dedicate your personality to God it will make you rejoice. Other people will notice it, just as the people from "afar off" noticed the joy of God's people on this day of dedication. People will see you and say, "Why is he so happy? I wish I could be that happy."

It is very important that every day we say, "God, I dedicate my personality and my reactions to You. I want You to react through me today." If you do not dedicate your personality and your reactions, then the devil can steal back some of the territory that you have gained.

When you begin to lose your temper, feel offended or get depressed, then you need to pray quickly, "God, my personality is Yours." Then your personality won't end up in defeat. You will be acting like God, and God always wins.

I want to look back at a story from the book of 2 Samuel. This is a story that contrasts two personalities, that of King David and his counselor, Ahithophel. King David's mistakes stand out as having been far worse than any of Ahithophel's mistakes, yet King David still ended up as a winner. Ahithophel, however, ended up in death and defeat because he did not close the gates of his personality to the enemy.

Ahithophel's name means "brother of folly," but in the beginning of his life he did not look like a man of folly. He looked like a very brilliant man who was a counselor to the king of Israel. King David loved, admired and respected this man very deeply. I wondered, "How could a man like Ahithophel end up being a traitor?" I looked more closely at his family and circumstances and came to some very interesting conclusions.

I found out that Ahithophel was the grandfather of a woman named Bathsheba. I know how fathers feel about their daughters; but if ever a girl is adored, it is by her grandfather! Bathsheba was probably raised well, and her parents must have been very selective in choosing her husband. Her husband Uriah turned out to be such a dedicated, turned-on Jew that any father would have been proud to have him as a son-in-law.

One evening David looked outside his palace from a roof-top and saw Bathsheba bathing herself nearby. The Bible tells you that this incident happened at a time when kings went to war. The rest of Israel's men were ar war, and that is where David should have been. But because he was spending time in idleness, he ended up sending for Bathsheba and committing adultery with her. It was not long afterward that David discovered Bathsheba was pregnant with his child.

David immediately sent for Bathsheba's husband Uriah. If Uriah went home and slept with Bathsheba, he would think that she was expecting his child. But when Uriah came home he was so devoted to his duty at war that he refused to go home to his wife. He said, *"The servants of my lord are encamped in the open fields; shall I then go into mine house, to eat and to drink, and to lie with my wife? as thou livest, and as thy soul liveth, I will not do this thing?"* (2 Samuel 11:11). If anything ever made David feel guilty, it was Uriah's words. David sent Uriah back to battle and ordered him to fight in the front line so that he was killed. Now David was guilty of murder as well as adultery.

After Uriah's death the Lord sent a prophet named Nathan to David. "You are really going to suffer for your sin. And Bathsheba's child is going to die."

Until this time Ahithophel had not been aware of David's involvement with Bathsheba. But when Nathan's prophecy exposed the truth, it must have deeply hurt Ahithophel. I am sure that bitterness rooted and began to grow in his heart. Yet he walked carefully before King David and never provoked him in any way. As Ahithophel walked, he was waiting for an opportunity to take revenge for the honor of his grand-daughter.

Apparently Ahithophel found his opportunity in turning his support away from David to David's son, Absalom. Absalom was a handsome, brilliant young man who made David very proud. The Bible says that from the sole of his foot to the crown of his head, Absalom did not have one blemish.

He had so much hair that every year when it was cut off, the cut hair weighed two to four pounds. You talk about women being vain—I think that's the heighth of vanity! I thought, "God, why did you waste all that wonderful hair on a man?"

But while David adored his son, apparently the feeling was not mutual. Absalom was so full of pride that eventually he decided he would make a better king than his father. Second Samuel 15:1 tells you that Absalom would sit by the gates of the city and win the hearts of the people to himself:

"And Absalom said unto him, See, thy matters are good and right; but there is no man deputed of the king to hear thee. Absalom said moreover, Oh that I were made judge in the land, that every man which hath any suit or cause might come into me, and I would do him justice" (2 Samuel 15:3,4).

As the townspeople passed by the city gate, Absalom talked to them and said, "My father doesn't really care about what's going on. He's out of touch, but I'm not. If I were the king, I would help you." The Bible tells you that Absalom "stole the hearts" of the people of Israel. David had no idea that his authority as king was being usurped by his own son, but I can guarantee you that Ahithophel was very aware of what was happening.

One day Absalom finally pronounced himself to be the king, and the kingdom of Israel was divided in its loyalties. Half of the kingdom still favored their former king, David. But the rest of the people's hearts were with Absalom. As soon as Absalom announced his kingship, David had to flee from the city to protect his life. And as soon as David fled, Ahithophel was at Absalom's side offering counsel.

Absalom's other counselor was a man named Hushai, who still favored David secretly. He was with Absalom, but he was masquerading his loyalty in order to protect David. When Absalom asked Ahithophel how David should be dealt with, Ahithophel said, "Let me choose 12,000 men. We will pursue David and all his people." Then Ahithophel added, *"I will smite the king only"* (2 Sam. 17:2).

When I read this I think, "Ahithophel, you're really in a hurry to kill David!"

Why would the king's own counselor want to murder the man for whom he worked? Because the thought had been brewing in his heart for years. Now Ahithophel's big opportunity for revenge had come, and when he spoke, it was, "Murder, murder, murder."

But Absalom was not content simply to take Ahithophel's advice without getting a second opinion. He asked Hushai his opinion and Hushai said, "Don't go tonight because David's men are angry and upset. They will be ready for blood."

Absalom preferred Hushai's counsel to that of Ahithophel and decided to wait before pursuing David. But the rejection of his own counsel was more than Ahithophel could bear. The Bible tells you that in his sorrow over having his counsel rejected, Ahithophel rode to his home and committed suicide by hanging himself.

This is not the end of the story. In the search for David Absalom followed behind his army of men. As he rode along, his beautiful hair was caught in the branches of a tree. The donkey rode out from under Absalom and left him hanging still alive between heaven and earth. David had instructed his men, "Don't kill Absalom, whatever you do." But I think that Joab, the leader of David's army, killed Absalom because he had heard of Absalom's entrapment in the tree. After Absalom was murdered, news was brought to David, and it grieved him deeply. There was no malice in the words he spoke: *"O my son Absalom, my son, my son Absalom! would God I had died for thee, O Absalom, my son, my son!"* (2 Samuel 18:33b).

I looked at David's character and saw no bitterness toward the son who had wanted to kill his own father. I saw no bitterness in David toward Ahithophel, who had been revengeful and a traitor. David had once been responsible for adultery and the murder of the woman's husband. Ahithophel, as far as I know, never did either. But he ended up committing suicide. David, the ex-adulterer and ex-murder, was taken back across the Jordan and was restored as Israel's king.

I would say that David's personality seemed to fail more times than did Ahithophel's personality. But Ahithophel did not guard his gates against the enemy. He let bitterness, hatred and revenge come in. The gates of his personality were closed to God, but they were open to the enemy's plans of dissension. Because of these things, Ahithophel died a broken man, while David came back as a winner.

David was willing to expose his personality to God, even when he was wrong. When Nathan prophesied to David, "There is sin in your life," David said, "That is exactly right.

I'm a sinner. I'm an adulterer and a murderer." The Bible says that the person who covers his sin will not prosper. (Proverbs 28:13). But the person who repents of sin brings in God's forgiveness and cleansing. True, David made mistakes, but he was a repenter—a man after God's own heart. He kept his personality dedicated to God, regardless of his mistakes along the way.

David wrote a psalm about Ahithophel, and it was eventually quoted by the Messiah Himself:

"For it was not an enemy that reproached me; then I could have borne it: neither was it he that hated me that did magnify himself against me; then I would have hid myself from him: But it was thou, a man mine equal, my guide, and mine acquaintance. We took sweet counsel together, and walked unto the house of God in company. Let death seize upon them, and let them go down quick into hell: for wickedness is in their dwellings, and among them. As for me, I will call upon God; and the Lord shall save me" (Psalm 55:12-16).

Ahithophel could have called on God and repented that night when he gave bad counsel to Absalom. He could have confessed his sin to God and not ended up in suicide. Through all the ages Ahithophel is not remembered as being a wise man, but is known as having been defeated because he allowed the gates of his personality to be broken down by the enemy.

You might say, "He had a right to be bitter." As Christians we have no right to be bitter. We have no right to hate. The only right we have is that of allowing Jesus Christ to react through us. I thought, "Ahithophel, what a shame that you ended up as a brother of folly, just like the meaning of your name!"

David's openness was so pleasing to God that He said, "David, your throne will never end." And David ended up in the lineage of our Lord Jesus Christ.

Oh, the importance of dedicating our personalities daily to God, so that bitterness may not enter our lives! David dedicated his personality to God, and it was worth it. You can be a king or you can be a spiritual suicide. Which will you choose? Choose to be a king and a priest.

"Create in me a clean heart, O God; and renew a right spirit within me. Cast me not away from thy presence; and take not thy holy spirit from me. Restore unto me the joy of thy salvation; and uphold me with thy free spirit" *(Psalm 51:10-12).*

(A psalm of David when Nathan the prophet came unto him.)

Chapter Seven

GOD CAN STABILIZE AN UNSTABLE PERSONALITY

Have you ever known Christians who had a specific call of God on their lives, yet they were up one minute and down the next? Whether you realize it or not, all of us have a specific call, whether or not it is in the full-time ministry. And just as all of us are called to a divine plan, all of us are too familiar with the frustration that Paul described in Romans 7:15, *"That which I do I allow not: for what I would, that do I not; but what I hate, that do I."*

Have you ever done something that you just hated—yet you did it anyway? Those are areas of instability in our lives where God wants to perform a transformation. I want to see how God took a person who, as far as appearances were concerned, "blew it" in every part of what God had for him. We might look at such a person today and say, "Wow, he really needs counseling. He has big problems!"

In studying the life of Samson, you will see how, even though he had a marvelous call of God on his life, he made some big mistakes. Yet God redeemed Samson's unstable personality in the end, just as God wants to redeem unstable areas in our own personalities.

In Judges 13 it tells you that an angel came to a woman from the tribe of Dan and brought her a wonderful message:

"Behold now, thou art barren, and bearest not: but thou shalt conceive, and bear a son" (Judges 13:3a).

As the woman listened to the angel's message, she was told, "You are not to drink wine or strong drink, or touch any unclean thing. From the time he is conceived in your womb, he will be a Nazarite unto God."

The Nazarite vow was for people to set themselves apart to God for certain periods of time, usually 60 to 90 days. During that time the person would not drink anything of an alcoholic nature, touch anything unclean, or cut his hair.

Basically the angel, sent to the woman of the tribe of Dan, was saying that her son be set apart with God's call on his life, from the moment of conception. He was to observe the Nazarite vow, not for 60 or 90 days, but for the span of his entire life.

In order for Samson to have been separated to God from the time of conception, his mother had to observe the Nazarite vow from the moment she received the angel's message to the time of Samson's birth. For the nine months she observed the Nazarite vow.

Upon hearing the angel's message from the Lord, the woman became very excited. The Bible doesn't tell her age, but I have a feeling that she was middle-aged and was previously unable to bear children. She ran to tell her husband about the angelic visitation, and he had a really great response: *"O my Lord, let the man of God which thou didst send come again unto us, and teach us what we shall do unto the child that shall be born"* (Judges 13:8).

The father-to-be, Manoah, said, "We need to know how to raise this special child!" He was really excited, because the angel had promised that this child would be a deliverer of Israel from the Philistines.

At this point in time Israel was being overwhelmed and oppressed by the Philistine nation a people who were from the Mediterranean coast of southern Israel. The Philistines were a very strong and aggressive nation who infiltrated the tribes of Israel and slowly overcame them. The Israelite government was squelched by the new Philistine government, which was very authoritarian. The people of Israel were not even allowed to have any metal with which to make weapons. The few knives given to the Israelites had to be sharpened in Philistine supervision. There were no swords, and even ordinary work tools were monitored. This was a very difficult and trying time for Israel, so the angelic prophecy of a deliverer was exciting news!

Evidently the woman prayed and was answered, and God sent the angel a second time to emphasize again the Nazarite vow. The woman then offered a gift, and the angel wondrously disappeared in a flame of fire.

When the child was born, the woman chose **Samson** for his name. Samson means "sunlike," because this child would bring light into a very dark situation. Not only was his important birth prophesied to his parents by an angel, but it was also prophesied in Genesis chapter 49. Jacob prophesied over his son, Dan, and spoke of one who would "judge his people." According to the Old Testament the only judge who came from the tribe of Dan was Samson. As you can see, he was a very important part of Israel's destiny.

After Samson's birth, the Lord blessed him. Then Judges

13:25 tells you that the Spirit of the Lord began to move upon Samson in the camp of Dan between Zorah and Eshtaol. The Hebrew wording for the Spirit "moving upon" Samson is very unusual. It is not the same thing as when we say, "The Lord moved upon my heart to do this." Rather, the Spirit of the Lord actually "broke in upon" Samson with special anointings of strength. Why an anointing of strength? Because God was calling Samson to be a one-man army for Israel!

So far you've seen Samson's positive characteristics, but he had his negatives, too. For one thing, Samson liked the wrong kind of women. The Bible tells you about three women to whom he was attracted, and they were all Philistines. That in itself was bad news for someone with a calling like Samson's! It's just like the devil to dress up sin in an attractive package to lure people from their callings. The Philistines were an evil people, and Samson was supposed to begin to deliver his people from them—not get involved with their women! But as soon as the Bible tells you about Samson's anointings, it also reveals his weaknesses.

It is always a shock to see a person who is very anointed of God having strong personality problems. Samson's first major mistake came in Judges 14:1 when he *"saw a woman in Timnath of the daughters of the Philistines."* Samson immediately fell in love and decided to marry the woman. But when he told his parents about his decision, of course, they were very distraught. You say, "Why wouldn't they be upset when their son wants to marry the daughter of an enemy tribe?" Yet, interestingly enough, Judges 14:4 tells you, *"His father and his mother knew not that it was of the Lord."* God could have used even this situation for His glory.

Having told his parents about his love for the Philistine

woman, Samson headed off for Timnath. On his way a tremendous anointing of strength came upon Samson, when a lion came out to roar against him. The Spirit came upon Samson, and he ripped the lion apart as though it were a little goat. You see, Samson was entering Philistine territory, and he needed to know that God was giving him an anointing to take him through.

An anointing is not only given from God so that you can carry out His plans for your life. It is also given to cover weaknesses in your personality so that you can be strong in Him. God wanted Samson to be strong in his personality when he encountered the Philistine people, but Samson did not realize it at all.

Samson's marriage feast was arranged in Timnath, and then you see a second weakness pop up in his personality: his love for practical jokes. Some people go through stages of practical joking, but Samson never seemed to outgrow it. At his wedding feast he told a riddle and said, "Anyone who knows the answer will receive 30 sheets and 30 changes of clothes."

Maybe Samson figured out that if he didn't get sheets and clothes as wedding gifts, he could get them through making this bet with the other men. Maybe he just wanted new clothes for his honeymoon. Whatever the case, Samson was sure that nobody would guess this riddle: "Out of the eater came forth meat, and out of the strong came forth sweetness."

Three days passed, and nobody could guess the answer to Samson's riddle. Samson wasn't the Philistines' favorite person anyway, because he was an Israelite. But it infuriated the men that they could not guess his riddle. Finally they approached his wife-to-be with threats, "If you don't find out the answer we'll burn your parents' house." She was so fearful that she began using every possible means to pry the answer to the riddle from Samson. "Oh, Samson, if you love me, you will tell me the answer."

Samson finally gave his wife-to-be the riddle answer: *"What is sweeter than honey? and what is stronger than a lion?"* (Judges 14:16). The girl then told it to her people, and when the men brought the answer to Samson, he was furious! At that moment the Spirit of the Lord broke in upon him. In a burst of anointed strength Samson went to Ashkelon, slew 30 men and stole their possessions for the men who had guessed the riddle.

While Samson was in Ashkelon, the Philistines gave his wife-to-be away to his companion. When Samson returned to Timnath, the girl's father said, "Sorry, but I already gave her away in marriage. Take her younger sister instead."

This is where Samson really became upset. Remember, it was his nature to play pranks. The next thing he did was to take 300 foxes and tie their tails together, two by two, with firebrands. Then he sent the foxes into some Philistine wheat fields and burned them to the ground.

Can you imagine just catching those foxes and tying their tails together? Why not just set fire to the wheat fields? Because a true prankster would be more creative! But the sad part of this story was the revenge. The Philistines went to the home of the woman whom Samson had intended to marry, killed her and her family, and burned their house down with fire. She had moved against Samson in fear for her life, but eventually she was killed anyway. Now Samson had a great thirst for vengeance.

After this tragic sequence of events Samson moved to a place called Etam. While he was living there, the Philistines, knowing the fear they invoked in the people of Israel, went to Samson's people and asked where he was. They said, "Bring Samson to us, or we will kill you off like flies."

The Israelites didn't back Samson at all. Instead, 3,000 men of Judah went after Samson and said, "We came to bind you up so that we can deliver you to the Philistines." Samson allowed them to bind him up. When the Philistines saw him they thought, "We've got him now." They were ready to kill him. But the Bible says that at that moment the Spirit of the Lord broke in mightily upon Samson, and he threw off the cords as though they were nothing. Then he found the jawbone of an ass, with which he killed 1,000 Philistine men.

I partially blame Israel for Samson's inability to handle his weaknesses. Remember that, outside of his parents' support, Samson stood alone. Never do you see Israel standing supportively behind him. In fact, the moment threats came to them, they delivered Samson to the enemy themselves!

How many times has God called a person and anointed him, yet been unable to find a person willing to pray for him? Instead of backing the person, his congregation bound him by picking him to pieces with criticism. Israel saw Samson's weaknesses, as well as his strengths, but didn't back him in either. The only thing the Israelites cared about was how they could benefit in any situation.

When Samson had killed 1,000 Philistine men, the people were thrilled with him and appointed him as a judge. For 20 years Samson judged Israel consistently. He was a good judge, and the Bible says nothing negative about how he handled the job. But sometimes if things aren't really exciting, or they're too much the same, we can get bored. The enemy comes along and says, "Take a spiritual vacation. Live it up and nobody will know."

Samson still had a yearning for a Philistine woman—the wrong kind of woman. The weakness hadn't been corrected. Samson had not dealt with his weaknesses, but he had not lost the anointing of God, either.

Then one day Samson went to a place called Gaza and became involved with a harlot. When the Philistines found out about Samson's involvement with this harlot, they really harrassed him about it. Finally Samson had taken his fill of harrassment, so he decided that it was time for another practical joke. This time he arose early one morning, went to Gaza's main entrance, pulled off the entire huge gate and set it on a hill, for spite. Here it was—twenty years later, and Samson was still pulling pranks!

The next morning when the Philistines found that the city gate had been placed up on a hill, they didn't have to ask who had done it. They knew that Samson had been the culprit.

You would think that after such mischief, Samson might have been smart enough not to get too closely involved with the Philistines. But immediately he went again into Philistine territory, and this time he became involved with another woman. Really this woman was well-described in the book of Proverbs, which says, "The adultress hunts for the precious life." An adultress isn't just selling her body for a piece of bread or a new dress. She is a woman with a plot and is after everything that a man owns.

This is a picture of a woman whose name was Delilah, and her name means "languishing." You know, the "southern belle" type, who says, "I'm so feminine...I'm so dependent." But she wasn't dependent at all! She was a cool one.

As soon as the Philistine men discovered that Samson was seeing Delilah, they came to Delilah and said, "Each of us will give you 1,100 pieces of silver if you find out the secret of Samson's strength.'' Six men told Delilah that they would each give her 1,100 pieces of silver! That would have been 6,600 pieces of silver—a lot of money in any economy! It was a lot of money to Delilah, and it was the precious life that she was seeking.

Delilah was not in love with Samson. She was in love with money. She knew that Samson was physically attracted to her, and she used that attraction as her weapon against him. One day she said, "Oh, Samson, I wish you would tell me how you can be so strong."

He said, "Well, if you bind me with brand new ropes, that will do it." So one night Delilah put Samson to sleep, bound him with rope and then yelled, "Samson, the Philistines are upon you!" Samson awakened instantly, breaking out of the ropes with ease. When he realized what Delilah had done, he laughed. After all, he was a prankster who loved a good joke.

Samson would only tease Delilah about the secret of his strength. Once he told her that if she bound him with green cords, he would be as weak as other men. That night Delilah tied green cords around Samson as he slept and then cried, "The Philistines be upon you, Samson!" Before the "Philistines" could take Samson, he broke the cords "like a thread."

Delilah made up her mind, "I have to be **more** helpless and **more** languishing," and she set herself to the task. "Samson, you really don't love me, or you would tell me the secret of your strength." She vexed him every day, "You just make fun of me, but you won't tell me the truth." The Bible says that finally Samson's soul was "vexed unto death," and he told Delilah the truth. He said, "I have been a Nazarite unto God from my mother's womb. If I am shaven, my strength will go from me.''

That night Delilah put Samson to sleep on her knees and called for a man who was waiting nearby with a razor. The seven locks of Samson's hair were shaven from his head, and then Delilah began to afflict Samson, ''The Philistines are upon you!'' When Samson arose, he did not realize that his anointing of strength was gone. The Philistine men took him away immediately and put out his eyes. He was taken to Gaza. I thought, ''Samson, your wandering eyes caused you to sin, and now they have been put out. You played cruel jokes in Gaza, and now you have become the joke.''

Samson was bound with fetters of brass and was made to work grinding corn in a prison house—a woman's work. While he was grinding corn, his hair slowly began to grow. But Samson's hair wasn't the only thing that was changing. His heart was also changing in repentance. To **repent** means to ''turn,'' so Samson was turning toward God again. His anointing was coming back.

One day the Philistines held a great feast for Dagon, their idol. Everybody became very drunk, so they called for Samson, to make a big joke of him. Some little boy led Samson out, since Samson could not see. Samson said, ''Lead me between the two pillars.'' The two pillars were the supports for the entire house in which the Philistines sat. All the major men of leadership were present on that day. So the little boy led Samson to the center of the two pillars where he could be seen by all.

Once he had taken his place, Samson prayed a beautiful prayer that showed his total personality turnaround:

> *''And Samson called unto the Lord, and said, O Lord*
> *God, remember me, I pray thee, and strengthen me, I*
> *pray thee, only this once, O God, that I may be at*

once avenged of the Philistines for my two eyes"
(Judges 16:28).

When Samson said, "O Lord God," he used God's name
Adonai, which means "Master." Then in that same statement he used the word **Jehovah,** or "Revealing One." Finally
when Samson said, "Oh God," he was using God's name
Elohim, meaning "Creator," or "Mighty One."

For the most part Samson had known God the way most
Christians know Him: as **Elohim,** and one who gives
strength. Samson also knew God as **Jehovah,** the one who
reveals His Holy Spirit and His personality to man. But Samson had never before made God the master and owner. Never
before had Samson said, "God, You call the shots. I will
obey." Samson had always called his own shots.

We can be filled with the Spirit, but if we don't allow God
to be more than our Savior, then our personalities will stay in
defeat. He is the one to whom we must submit our personalities. You don't have to hate your actions—the weak
areas of your personality—that betray your heart. You just
have to know God as **Adonai** or "Master."

Samson said, "Oh, God, **Let me** be avenged of the
Philistines." Not, "God, I'll do it," but "God, You do it."
Samson was fulfilling his call in God's way. He grasped the
two pillars, between which he stood, and prayed, "Let me die
with the Philistines." Samson pushed with an anointing of
strength on those pillars, and the entire house of Philistines
came crashing to the ground. Samson may have died with the
Philistines, but he went to a different place than they did.
The Bible tells you that Samson killed more Philistines in his
death than he killed during his whole life.

The family of Samson came for his body, which was buried
between Zorah and Eshtaol, the same place where the Spirit

first moved upon him. The Bible says, "Having begun in the Spirit, shall we end in the flesh?" Samson drifted away from the Spirit in the interim of his life, but he still ended in the Spirit, and you can too. He began in the Spirit, got in the flesh, but ended in the Spirit.

Let's remember that after our personalities have been dedicated to God, He wants to stay the Master over our weaknesses. Make God your Adonai, the divine Director and Master of your life's beginning, middle and end.

Chapter Eight

PERSONALITY CHANGE BRINGS APPETITE FOR THE WORD

It's exciting to know the impact that God's Word has on a personality that has been resurrected in Christ. It is so much greater than the impact on a personality that is up-and-down, in-and-out, and does not know its authority over Satan.

Nehemiah chapter eight is about the revival that God's Word brought to the people after they had dedicated their personalities to God. This chapter is one of the few in the Bible where the people could eat fat and drink sweet drinks. It's a chapter that is full of carbohydrates! Throughout the Bible, especially in Proverbs, you find many warnings about foods, such as, "Don't be a glutton" or "Don't eat too many sweets." But I think it's interesting that in the chapter about God's Word the people feasted on fats.

In this chapter, the walls of Jerusalem had been built, and her gates had been restored. The people were concerned, not with building anymore, but with hearing God's Word. In our lives, once the building has been done, God says, "Here is a personality that was restored by the Holy Spirit. Now it is ready to receive my Word in fullness through the Water Gate."

"And all the people gathered themselves as one man into the street that was before the water gate; and they spake unto Ezra the scribe to bring the book of the law of Moses as the Lord had commanded to Israel" (Nehemiah 8:1).

Notice that the people read God's Word by the Water Gate, because in your personality that is the gate through which you receive the Word. Once God's people began receiving the Word through this gate, they experienced revival. Why? Because if you love God's Word and have an expectancy toward it, you have reviving power!

The Israelites had a tremendous, positive attitude toward God's Word. First of all, you see that they **reverenced** it:

"And Ezra opened the book in the sight of all the people; (for he was above all the people;) and when he opened it, all the people stood up" (Nehemiah 8:5).

People whose personalities have been repaired by the Holy Spirit experience a new reverence and appreciation for God's Word. Nehemiah tells you that Ezra and the priests, however, did more than just read the Word—they explained what it meant to the people:

*"And the Levites, caused the people to understand the law: and the people stood in their place. So they read in the book of the law of God distinctly, and gave the sense, **and caused them to understand the reading**" (Nehemiah 8:7b,8).*

Basically, teaching God's Word is simply the practice of making it understandable to those hearing it, so that they can apply it to their lives. Ezra said, "It's great that you are listening to the Word, but you also have to receive it so that you can practice it in your lives." The Word is not just to be read. It is to be applied to everything we do!

I have found that a personality with a positive attitude toward God's Word is the one that receives the most from it:

> *"And Nehemiah, which is the Tirshatha, that taught the people, said unto all the people, this day is holy unto the Lord your God; mourn not, nor weep. **For all the people wept,** when they heard the words of the law" (Nehemiah 8:9).*

The children of Israel were so deeply touched by the Word of God that it moved them to weep. These people reverenced God's Word, so they began to understand it. Then the Word of God moved their hearts, first to tears, and then to great joy:

> *"Then he said unto them, Go your way, eat the fat, and drink the sweet, and send portions unto them for whom nothing is prepared: for this day is holy unto our Lord: neither be ye sorry; for the joy of the Lord is your strength" (Nehemiah 8:10).*

Hearing the Word brings joy to your heart! I love the words of Ezra: "Don't weep. Today is your day to be happy in the Word!" You know, many times in counseling I have come across people who have used the Word for condemnation rather than conviction and help. But God did not send His Word to condemn us. He sent it to convict and convince us that He truly loves us.

The priests described in Nehemiah said, "Don't mourn. Don't be put down by the Word. Let it lift up and fill your heart with joy.''

So many times we have sung, "The joy of the Lord is my strength." We just love that little chorus. But have we realized where the joy of the Lord and our strength are found? They are found in His Word. God's Word was meant to be our direct source of joy. Any man, woman or child who gets involved in the Word will be involved in joy. Any person who reverences the Word is going to start rejoicing. Any person who respects and worships the Word will find that the joy of the Lord is his strength.

But Ezra did not just say, "Go and be joyful." He said, "Send portions to others." In other words, "Share what you have." We as Christians are supposed to enjoy the sweetness of God's Word. But God says, "Don't just be a hog about the Word and not do anything else. Send it to people who don't have it."

When you share the Word of God with other people, you receive even more joy. You cannot share Jesus without experiencing increased joy. I have observed that in my personal life I love my quiet study time in God's Word. But then God wants to **complete** my joy by causing me to share His Word with others. He also wants to allow me to see His Word work in other people's lives.

You say, "I'm joyful because I had a wonderful answer to prayer." Yes, but that is only temporary joy. God's Word brings permanent joy. Once in Billings, Montana, a Methodist woman at one of my meetings received Christ as her savior. Afterward she came to me and said, "My husband is in the hospital. Do you ever make hospital calls to pray for people?"

I told her, "I would be happy to pray for him."

I found out that the woman's husband had been a senator. One day during a senate meeting he had fallen backward to the floor, was taken to a hospital, and there his surgeons discovered that he had a brain tumor. The woman said, "He is in a coma and the doctors doubt that his condition will ever improve."

The devil said to me, "If you pray for him he will die. You need Oral Roberts or Kathryn Kuhlman for this. You need someone who is really powerful in God. Who are you?"

I fixed my thoughts on Mark 16:18, *"They [believers] shall lay hands on the sick and they shall recover."* I thought "God's Word says that when believers lay hands on sick people, they **will** recover. It's my part to lay hands on people. God will take care of the rest."

When I arrived at the man's hospital room, his appearance was really sad. His eye was bandaged and there were tubes in his nose. I laid my hands on the man and commanded the spirits of death to leave. Then I prayed that the man's healing would bring glory to the name of Jesus.

When I prayed for the woman's husband to be healed, the devil said, "You didn't have faith when you prayed." But I just clung to Mark 16:18. I said, "God says that when I lay hands on sick people, they will recover." I left the hospital room and returned home the following day.

Just one month later the woman who had asked me to pray for her husband called me to say, "My husband's health has done a complete turnaround since you prayed." He was no longer comatose. The man was eating, drinking, walking, and all of his bodily functions near normal.

Jesus is so good! He wants to do more than just save our bodies—He also wants to save our souls. That autumn my husband and I traveled back to Billings, Montana, and Wally visited the man for whom I had prayed. He was still in the hospital, so as Wally sat with him and read scriptures aloud. On that day the man accepted Christ, right there in the hospital bed! Today, the man travels, works, and is growing spiritually.

What brought life into that man's heart and physical body? The Word, the Word, the Word! Revival never fails to flow when you share God's Word with other people.

You may say, "I have revival, and my personality has already been repaired." But you need a **continuous** input of God's Word inside. Sometimes the devil comes to knock holes in the walls of your personality. He tries to throw fiery darts at your gates of authority to catch them on fire. But when God's Word is constantly flowing through your life, its refreshing overwhelms enemy fire. Only through continuing in God's Word will you advance from one victory to the next. Only then can you enjoy the abundance of benefits intended for you in the Word.

As I ended my study on the Israelites' revival near the Water Gate, the Lord said, "The revival took place in the first week of the seventh month, and seven is the number of completion. My Word brought the people completion in their personalities."

If you need a revival of joy inside, feast on the Word of God! In it you will find a river of consistent joy that can complete any area of your life:

"He that is of a merry heart hath a continual feast"
(Proverbs 15:15).

Chapter Nine

RESURRECTION BREAD TO FEED YOUR PERSONALITY

Sometimes we look at ourselves and say, "I'll never change. My mother and father were failures, and I'll be a failure." Then we pull out a long, long list of what we are and what we are not. But if you are a Christian who is feeding on the Word of God, then you can receive resurrection power to make your personality rise above failure just as Jesus rose from death into the heavenlies.

Resurrection power is one of the most exciting things that God has for your personality. You received it when you were born again, and it was given to you for the purpose of transforming your soul. No wonder that Philippians 2:13 can say, *"It is God which worketh in you, both to will and to do his good pleasure."* His work of ressurection within you delights Him and benefits you.

I never gave much thought to resurrection power until a woman shared with me her revelation on what the Bible says about leavened and unleavened bread. Her words so provoked me that I couldn't wait to get home to look up the references!

You may wonder, "What in the world does bread have to do with my personality?" It has a lot to do with your personality! You are going to be thrilled at how God has put resurrection power at work in your spirit for your soul—your personality—and your body. You can see a picture of that work in both the Old and New Testaments.

On the night when the Israelites departed from Egypt, they ate unleavened bread with a lamb that had been roasted by fire. Before that first Passover meal, all leaven had been removed from the house of every Hebrew person. In this case, and in many cases in the Bible, the unleavened bread was representative of sinlessness. The people were to clean the sin from their lives before God could move on their behalf.

Not only did God have the people eat unleavened bread at the time of their exodus from Egypt, but also they ate unleavened bread when God began giving commands about sacrifices. Any blood from sacrifices was to be offered with unleavened bread because God did not want sin involved in them.

In the New Testament Jesus said, *"I am the bread of life"* (John 6:35a). We all know that Jesus said those words about Himself, but how often do we relate His words to the incident in which He multiplied five loaves and two fish to feed 5,000 people? First Jesus multiplied the food. Then He fed the multitudes and told them, "I am the bread of life."

> *"Verily, verily, I say unto you, Moses gave you not that bread from heaven; but my Father giveth you the true bread from heaven" (John 6:32).*

I was sure that in this passage of scripture, Jesus must have been talking about unleavened bread. But to my shock, when I studied the Greek, He was speaking of leavened bread! That bread has yeast in it. Does leavened bread come from heaven? I thought that perhaps in my study there had been an error, so I quickly referred back to the Old Testament to look up some more scriptures. I thought, "Lord, where did they eat leavened bread as opposed to unleavened bread?" I found out that in the Old Testament there were two times when leavened bread was to be eaten by the people of Israel.

Amos 4:5 says, *"Offer a sacrifice of thanksgiving with leaven, and proclaim and publish the free offerings: for this liketh you, O ye children of Israel, saith the Lord God."*

When the sons of Israel made a thanksgiving offering, in which they thanked God for all His works in their lives, their offering contained leaven. I thought, "How interesting that offerings of thanks have rising power!"

Looking further, I found that on the day of Pentecost, two huge loaves of bread were baked for the feast day, and those loaves contained leaven. God said, "When you give thanksgiving, and when you celebrate Pentecost, use leavened bread."

Why use leaven if it is a type of sin? The study was beginning to confuse me, more than make sense, so I studied further in the New Testament to see what God had to say about leavened bread. One positive scripture was a parable in Matthew:

"The kingdom of heaven is like unto leaven, which a woman took, and hid in three measures of meal, till the whole was leavened" (Matthew 13:33).

We can't say there is anything wrong with the kingdom of heaven, can we? God wouldn't compare the kingdom of heaven with a type of sin.

I found out that there is more than one type of leaven. In

Luke 12:1 Jesus said, *"Beware the leaven of the Pharisees,"* and indicated again that leaven is a type of sin—in this case that of wrong doctrine. But there is a right kind of leaven that has rising power to cause a Christian's life to flourish and be fruitful. The right kind of leaven will increase the work of God in your life. But the wrong kind of leaven will increase the devil's work.

When the devil places leaven in a man's heart, whether it is false doctrine or some other kind of sin, that sin begins to spread. Sin doesn't stop with "one little tiny sin." It multiplies into more. That is why it is so important that our members be dedicated to works of righteousness every day.

In 1 Corinthians 5:7, Paul exhorted his brethren, *"Purge out therefore the old leaven, that ye may be a new lump."* He was speaking of immorality in the church—the devil's leaven.

Paul, however, knew the power of heavenly leaven. In Acts 27, he was sailing on a ship with unbelievers when a terrible storm threatened to overwhelm them all. Paul called all the people together and said, "We could die in shipwreck, so let's fast." The other people on the ship were unbelievers, yet they all fasted with Paul so that God would save them! When the storm subsided, everyone broke their fast and, by Paul's recommendation, ate meat for sustenance. But it is interesting that Paul did not eat meat. Instead, he ate leavened bread.

I believe that Paul, in eating leavened bread, was making a statement: "I am taking the bread of Jesus Christ that brings me resurrection power." If you're wondering how I can make that conclusion, I found it in John 6:32,33.

Jesus spoke of Himself, *"My Father giveth you the true bread from heaven.* ***For the bread of God is he which cometh down from heaven and giveth life unto the world."*** Jesus

Christ is our leavened bread to give us divine life!

I wondered, "What kind of bread did Jesus give His disciples in the Last Supper?" The scripture says, *"And he [Jesus] took bread, and gave thanks, and brake it, and gave unto them, saying, This is my body which is given for you: this do in remembrance of me"* (Luke 22:19). In the Last Supper, Jesus gave His disciples leavened bread. It represented His body, which would rise from the grave in only a few days to give life to the world. He was saying, "I am going to die, but I am going to rise, and through my death you will eat of my resurrection."

John 6:50 says, *"This is the bread which cometh down from heaven that a man may eat thereof and not die."* When you eat of Jesus, the bread of life, you eat of resurrection power and will never taste eternal death.

In Mark chapter seven a woman whose daughter had an unclean spirit came and fell at Jesus' feet to ask for His mercy on the daughter:

> *"The woman was a Greek, a Syrophenician by nation; and she besought him that he would cast forth the devil out of her daughter. But Jesus said unto her, Let the children first be filled: for it is not meet to take the children's bread, and to cast it unto the dogs"* (Mark 7:26,27).

What kind of bread was Jesus speaking of in this text? He was talking about leavened bread. What is the "children's bread?" It is resurrection power! The children of God must have the bread of life if their lives are to put forth the resurrection power of God to help others. That life in them causes healing and transformation for others.

The disciples learned the power of resurrection through leavened bread as they tarried together before Pentecost:

"And they continued stedfastly in the apostles' doctrine and fellowship, and in breaking of bread, and in prayers" (Acts 2:42).

The disciples were partaking of leavened bread because they were esteeming the resurrection of Christ. The more they ate of Jesus, the more resurrection power filled the room!

There was a feast of unleavened bread in the New Testament, but there was also a very strong revelation of the importance of leavened bread. It is so important that we esteem the leaven of the kingdom that God has placed to grow and multiply in our hearts. As resurrection power grows in our hearts, it reaches forth and extends that power to those around us.

In 1 Corinthians chapter 10, Paul unfolded a very deep revelation about partaking of resurrection bread when we take communion:

"The cup of blessing which we bless, is it not the communion of the blood of Christ? The bread which we break, is it not the communion of the body of Christ? For we being many are one bread, and one body: for we are all partakers of that one bread" (1 Corinthians 10:16,17).

Hold on to your seat, because I always used to think that the bread of communion was unleavened bread. But I don't believe that anymore. I believe that we are to take leavened bread, because the taking of communion is to bring resurrection power into our lives! When you take communion, you have the benefit of bringing supernatural life into your mind, your body, and your soul—your personality. Jesus wanted that power to fill your whole being!

After His resurrection Jesus appeared to His disciples and

caused them to catch a net of fish so great that they could not pull the net from the water. On the shore of the ocean, as Jesus cooked the fish over a fire, He also gave His disciples bread. Peter had returned to the fishing trade and had taken all the disciples with him. All of them had absolutely left behind the work of the gospel and were following Jesus to become fisherman again. That seems like a terrible thing to do, but Jesus knew how to bring them back: He gave them the bread of resurrection power!

Peter had been struggling on the fishing boat all night and had not caught one single fish. We really know how to struggle, don't we? Then a man stood on the shore saying, "Children." The word for "children," is **pedagogue,** indicating a child who is in training. The man called, "Have you anything to eat?"

The disciples shouted back, "No, we worked all night and didn't catch a thing."

Jesus called back, "Cast your nets to the other side." The disciples still didn't recognize Him, but they did as He had said. You see, sometimes a person standing ashore can spot the darkened areas of the water where entire schools of fish are swimming. When the disciples cast their nets on the other side, there were so many fish that they hardly knew what to do! At that moment Peter recognized that the man on the shore was Jesus.

When Peter saw Jesus, he grabbed the whole load of fishes and hauled it to the shore by himself! Somehow, in the presence of Jesus, Peter could do what six men could not. Peter was tasting of resurrection power. Peter had been very defeated, and at that point in his life, all he could see was failure. He had denied Jesus, so then he wondered, "What's the use of going on? I'm no disciple." Have you ever felt that way? Have you blown it royally, and now you wonder, "Why bother?" Jesus wants to lift you out of that depression and bring you into resurrection power for your personality.

When Peter came to the shore, Jesus didn't say, "Peter, I just wanted to talk about how you denied Me. Not only did you deny Me, but you returned to the fishing trade and left the ministry to which I called you." Jesus didn't reprove Peter. Instead, Jesus led Peter into resurrection power to transform his life.

Jesus said, "Peter, I fixed you a meal." Peter was cold from the spray of the water and tired from trying unsuccessfully all night to catch fish. He was hungry. He felt defeated. Jesus fed Peter and the rest of the disciples the fish they had caught. The Lord was concerned about their physical needs, as well as their spiritual needs. By feeding the disciples leavened bread, with the fish, Jesus was saying, "I am preparing you to participate in resurrection."

Then Jesus began to ask Peter some questions. Jesus said, "Peter, do you love Me?" Jesus was asking, "Peter, do you **agape** Me?" Agape is the kind of love with which God loves us. Peter answered, "Lord, You know I love you," and there the word **love** is "phileo," meaning the reciprocal love between friends. Peter was saying, "You love me, and I also love you."

Jesus told Peter, "Feed my sheep." Then He asked, "Peter, do you love [agape] Me ?"

Again, Peter said, "Lord, You know I love You."

Jesus said, "Feed My Lambs."

Then for a third time, Jesus asked Peter, "Do you love Me?" This time the word "love" that Jesus used was **phileo,** meaning "reciprocal love." Why did Jesus ask Peter three times? I think there are a number of factors involved here that show how Jesus led Peter back into resurrection power.

You see, Peter had denied the Lord three times, so Jesus asked three times, "Do you love Me?" The last time Peter had seen Jesus, Peter was warming his hands over the enemy's fire. Now, as he stood with Jesus by the fire, the memories certainly must have rushed back to Peter's mind. But Jesus hadn't come to put Peter down. Jesus wanted to bring leavened bread to make Peter rise above past defeats.

When Jesus used the word **phileo** (reciprocal love), He was saying, "Peter, you can feed My sheep even if you only love me reciprocally."

Why, then, did Jesus first emphasize agape love? Because those who are involved in feeding God's Word to the Body of Christ must expect nothing back. You may feed sheep who will turn against you, hate you, despise you and lie about you, as Judas did to the Lord. Despite those things, you still have to love in return. Only God's love, agape love, is capable of loving in that way.

Jesus was saying, "Peter, I am giving you resurrection bread because you will return to the ministry, and you will need rising power. You must love me with a love that expects nothing back." Then Jesus prophesied about the love that Peter would need to have:

"Verily, verily, I say unto thee, When thou wast young, thou girdedst thyself, and walkedst whither thou wouldest: but when thou shalt be old, thou shalt stretch forth thy hands, and another shall gird thee, and carry thee whither thou wouldest not" (John 21:18).

Jesus was saying, Peter, because of My resurrection power in you, you are going to love Me and the Body so greatly that you will be willing to die for them. Peter, somebody is going to take you where you don't want to go, and they will stretch out your hands." Historians say that Peter was crucified for his faith, and when the men crucified him, he said, "Don't crucify me like Jesus. I am not worthy to die like Him," so Peter was crucified upside-down. He had fed the Lord's sheep with agape love that expected nothing in great love.

Jesus ended His prophecy to Peter with the words, "Follow Me." How could Peter follow the Lord unto death, having denied him before? Peter had resurrection bread, so he had partaken of life and power.

Jesus placed His own life, resurrection power, in you when you were saved. Every time you take communion, remember that you are taking Jesus' life and ability to rise over any hindrances to your personality. You are taking resurrection power, the leavened bread of Christ.

Jesus doesn't want your personality to be defeated. Peter was defeated, but he came out of it so much that he was even martyred for the Lord. He then arose, victorious, into heavenly places with the Lord. That same victory in which Peter overcame is the victory that is in your heart and life through Jesus Christ. Let your personality rise into the Lord's high calling for you.

Chapter Ten

HOW YOUR PERSONALITY CAN DRAW INTEREST

In studying Nehemiah you have seen the importance of the gates of authority in your personality. You saw the hanging of the walls and the completion of the gates, but then you saw that even though completed, the city was still subject to attack. God says, "Just because the walls are up does not mean that you will never have another attack against your personality."

Then you looked at how dedication of your personality to God is important, including daily dedication to Him. We need to dedicate our actions and reactions so that we will handle every situation the way He wants us to handle it.

By now you have seen the necessary parts of bringing your personality together and keeping it yielded to God. But never forget that, throughout your life, God will deal with you continually in your personality. It is important to heed what He says.

Sometimes we think, "God isn't even bothering to deal with me." But He is. I saw this in the lives of Abraham and Sarah.

Thinking about Sarah always makes me chuckle because the Bible is very plain about the qualities of her humanity. Sarah wanted a baby so badly! In her day it was considered a disgrace to not have a baby, so I'm sure that pride was a part of the problem. But she also had a woman's natural desire for children. Sarah, though, was physically unable to have children.

God promised Sarah and Abraham a child, but for years that child didn't come. Being human and not having her personality totally submitted to God, Sarah patched up something that she imagined to be a terrific plan. She said, "Abraham, I have a great idea. Since I haven't had children, maybe God would use my handmaiden to give you a child. Then she could turn the child over to me, and it would be ours. This could be the child that God promised."

Abraham listened to this beautiful wife of his. The Bible tells you that she was really a knockout, she was so stunning. Sarah convinced him of her plan, and not long afterward, Hagar had Abraham's child.

After the child was born, Sarah was no longer excited about the idea. Instead, you find old, human Sarah. She was jealous. Of course she was jealous! Wouldn't you be jealous, if your husband had a child by some other woman, and they brought it to you to be raised—not to mention that the child would be a reminder of your husband's relationship with someone else!

Here were the child, Hagar, and Sarah all sharing the same kitchen. It doesn't work today, it didn't work then, and it wasn't in God's plan. Sarah really became tense with Hagar, and Hagar said, "I don't have to take this. After all, I had the baby."

That statement was like taking a cat and rubbing its fur

backwards. Sarah said, "Something has to be done about this. Abraham, get this woman out of here!"

Eventually a much more submissive Hagar was accepted back into Sarah's household. Finally the time arrived for Abraham and Sarah to have a child. Three divine visitors came to announce God's plan to Abraham, and he knew they were from God.

Meanwhile, Sarah was inside the tent eavesdropping. One of the visitors said to Abraham, "You are going to have a son," and inside the tent Sarah laughed aloud. She thought that it was hilarious because she and Abraham were both past the age of childbearing. They had no physical relationship any more, so how could there be a baby? Then the divine visitor asked Abraham, "Why did your wife laugh?" Sarah opened the tent door and said, "Oh, I didn't laugh." Just like a woman. But she did have the baby.

Hebrews 11 really compliments Sarah by saying that she had faith for the strength to have a baby. Don't say that Abraham had all the faith just because Sarah laughed. Sarah had faith for the strength she needed. I looked up the Greek word for **strength** and it is **dunamis,** or "miracle-working power." Sarah, in all her human frailty, also had faith. She had faith that God would give her a child, and He gave her a baby whose name was Isaac. I think that God really has a sense of humor because the child's name means "laughter." Maybe God said, "I had the last laugh, didn't I, Sarah? You laughed in unbelief, but I laugh because my promises really are true and real."

How good God is! How exciting and patient, because He takes us right where we are—just the raw material—and begins molding our personalities in spite of our failures. Aren't you glad that He never gives up?

However, although God does not give up, we can choose to live our lives in a constant battle by not allowing the Holy Spirit to lead and guide us. The enemy is always around, trying to lead us in a different direction than that of God. I looked at the life of a man named Eli and saw a tragedy that did not have to happen.

Eli was a spiritual man, but he did not stand against the devil's attacks. When he recognized and was warned about those attacks, he refused to do anything about them.

The name "Eli" is beautiful, for it means "My God." Eli was an outstanding priest who loved God's work and did not shirk priestly responsibilities. The people counseled with Eli, prayed with him, and he offered sacrifices for them. You say, "He sounds wonderful."

But you can be wonderful in your service to God and neglectful of the other areas of your life. We need to respond to whatever area God is dealing with, and in Eli's case the problem was with his two sons, Hophni and Phinehas.

When you see the names of Eli's two sons, you begin to see how important our dealings with our children are. I remember one time when I was having difficulty with my own young son, shortly after my husband and I adopted him. I prayed, "Lord, why have you given me a child when my attitude is so poor?" He said, "Marilyn, there are some things that I can only teach you through a child." That was a real shocker! Everyone who is a parent, however, will say "amen" to that 1,000 times!

Eli had two children whom God wanted to use in molding and shaping his personality. **Hophni** means "my first," and **Phinehas** means "mouth of pity." The first was a rebel, and the second was a whiner. I have seen both rebellion and whining in my own children, and I can't stand either of them.

But you can't ignore them. You have to deal with them. Eli, however didn't deal with the problems that his sons presented.

In the beginning of the book of First Samuel, a woman came to the temple where Eli ministered as a priest, and there was a great contrast between her and Eli. The woman, Hannah, had no children but desperately wanted them. She had a husband who adored her and would have done anything for her, but she was not satisfied with just his love. She wanted a baby.

Hannah's husband had another wife who had given him children, but the Bible tells you that he loved Hannah more than the other wife. Seemingly, Hannah just couldn't get over her childlessness, which the other wife would not let her forget.

One day, at the time of the yearly sacrifice, Hannah's husband, Elkanah, brought his wives and children to Shiloh, and when they arrived Hannah went to the temple. There she prayed silently, "God, give me a child." Her prayer was very specific:

> *"O Lord of hosts, if thou wilt indeed look on the affliction of thine handmaid, and remember me, and not forget thine handmaid, but wilt give unto thine handmaid a man child, then I will give him unto the Lord all the days of his life, and there shall no razor come upon his head" (1 Samuel 1:11).*

As Hannah prayed, she travailed so much that Eli walked over and said, *"How long wilt thou be drunken? put away thy wine from thee"* (1 Sam. 1:14). Hannah wasn't drunk, she was just upset. My first reaction to Eli's statement would be to tell him, "It's none of your business saying anything to Hannah, because you don't correct your own children. You correct a woman for drinking, but you won't correct your sons for doing the same thing!''

But I want you to see the unfolding of God's plan in these two personalities. One of the personalities was willing to respond to situations in God's way. The other was not. Eli was a priest, yet he refused God's dealings with his children. Hannah received the dealing of God.

When Eli had confronted Hannah, she answered, ''I'm not drunk. I'm sorrowful in spirit because I want a child.'' Then Eli spoke some words that were full of faith: *"Go in peace: and the God of Israel grant thee thy petition that thou hast asked of him" (1 Samuel 1:17).*

When Eli spoke those words, Hannah believed them. She went to eat at the feast of the peace offering with the rest of her family. The next morning, they rose up early to worship and then go home. Then the Lord said that Hannah conceived her child from the Lord that morning, and she had a beautiful little boy whom she named ''Samuel,'' meaning ''asked of God.''

Hannah said, ''I am going to keep this child until he is weaned, and then I will give him back to God. He will be loaned to God all his life.''

I looked at Hannah and thought, ''Imagine having just one child, one beautiful boy,'' which I imagine Samuel was. I thought, ''After Samuel was weaned, she gave that boy to Eli, who knew absolutely nothing about raising children.''

He let his boys rebel all their lives. When they became priests, they still rebelled by committing adultery with the women who sought spiritual counsel, by drinking strong drink, and eating the fat from the sacrifices.

How could Hannah send her gift from God into that

environment? From looking at natural circumstances we would say, "That's going to ruin Samuel's personality! He is so young and impressionable." But because Hannah had loaned Samuel to the Lord, Samuel was no longer her responsibility. He was God's responsibility, and God blessed him.

Hannah left her son at the temple with Eli, and she saw her child each year, when she brought him a new little coat that she had made for him. She was true to her vow, and the story shows that anything you give to God draws interest, because God gave Hannah five more children!

As Samuel grew, God began dealing with Eli, and of all people, God dealt with him through the child. One evening when Samuel was just a little boy, he heard a voice as he slept, "Samuel, Samuel!" The child thought that Eli was calling, so he ran to the priest and asked, "Did you call me?" Eli said, "I didn't call you. Go back to bed."

Samuel went back to bed, and then the voice spoke his name again. Again he asked the priest, "Did you call me?" Samuel received the same answer as before, so he went to sleep again. Again he heard the voice.

Eli was definitely a spiritually perceptive man. He had perceived faith in Hannah and told her to receive her son. Now he perceived that the voice Samuel heard was the Lord speaking to him. Eli told the child, "The next time you hear the voice, say, 'Speak, Lord, for thy servant heareth!'"

Samuel went back to his room, and when the voice spoke to him, "Samuel," he said, "Speak, Lord, for thy servant heareth." Instead of receiving a positive, uplifting message from the Lord, the first thing Samuel heard was negative!

"In that day I will perform against Eli all things which I have spoken concerning his house: when I begin, I will also make an end. For I have told him

that I will judge his house for ever for the iniquity which he knoweth; because his sons made themselves vile, and he restrained them not. And therefore I have sworn unto the house of Eli, that the iniquity of Eli's house shall not be purged with sacrifice nor offering for ever" (1 Samuel 3:12-14).

God was basically saying, "Eli honored his children above Me." How terrible it is that Eli put his children first! God is teaching us through our children, and God had warned Eli about his children before. Yet Eli ignored God's dealings and chose to let the boys go their own ways.

The morning after God spoke to Samuel, the boy woke up, not wanting to tell Eli what had been said. But Eli said, "What did God tell you? Don't hold anything back from me. I will not be angry with you."

Samuel said, "You put your children above God, so God is going to cut you off, and cut off your children from priesthood." This deeply saddened Samuel.

After this incident, Samuel really began to grow in the Lord and in ministry toward the people. Meanwhile, the Philistines came on the scene and began abusing the people of Israel, and the people were very backslidden. Eli had never corrected his sons, either. Spiritually, things looked bad, and everyone wondered what to do.

Everyone wants to get spiritual when they experience troubles. I am not against that, because trouble has brought many people to God. But we should get spiritual **before** trouble comes, and then maybe it won't be so troublesome!

The people said, "Let's get the ark of the covenant and take it into the Philistine camp." When the Philistines heard that the Israelites were bringing out the ark, they said, "God is come into the camp! Woe unto us!" (1 Sam. 4:7). The

Philistines knew that they would have to fight against Israel.

The Philistines raced out, fought hard, and won the battle against Israel. Eli's sons, Hophni and Phinehas, were killed, and it wasn't long before the news circulated back to Eli.

By this time Eli was a very fat old man. You may get mad at me for this, and if you do, I hope you'll forgive me; but I don't think that God ignores fat on our bodies. He is concerned when we don't discipline our physical bodies because it may indicate a lack of discipline in other areas in our lives.

When Eli heard about the news of his son's deaths, he then asked about the ark. The men reporting the news told Eli, "The ark was captured by the Philistines." Of course, Eli's prime concern was the ark of the covenant, which does give some credit to his spiritual desires. But if you won't let God move in all the areas of your personality, you can ruin the other areas. Upon hearing that the ark of the covenant had been taken, Eli fell over backward and broke his neck.

If you follow the line of Eli's priesthood further, you will find that God ended the entire priesthood from the lineage of Eli. He completely cut off that household because of the intentional overindulgence and disobedience that had taken place. Why? Because Eli would not allow God to have a certain area of his personality. God doesn't want our service. He wants our selves, and the service will be a fruit coming from our submission to God.

What happened to Samuel? He became the priest. He was a beautiful example of a priest, for he traveled, ministered and counseled the people. But then one day the people came to Samuel and said, "All the other nations have kings, but we have you, a prophet and priest. We want a king, too."

Listening to this, Samuel was hurt. Samuel brought the

hurt to God, and He said, "Don't take it personally. They haven't rejected you, they have rejected Me. If they want a king, let them have a king."

Samuel anointed a king named Saul, who never allowed his personality to be subjected to God. Saul was really a rebel! The walls and gates of his personality were full of holes, and he never listened to God. Finally, God dealt with Saul and said that the kingdom would be taken from him.

Even though Saul was such a selfish man, Samuel still loved him and said, "God forbid that I should ever cease to pray for you."

We want to say, "Samuel, this man took your place! He pushed you out of being the leader." But Samuel knew that the people hadn't rejected him. They had rejected God. And God never takes you from one position without giving you another. He gave Samuel the greatest ministry of his life by calling him to start a prophet's school.

Today when you read about all of the exciting prophets of the Old Testament, including Elijah, Elisha, and Nathan, all of them came from a school that was started by a prophet named Samuel.

Samuel returned to his home town, Ramah, and on the land he inherited from his parents, he stepped up in the plan of God. Hannah probably looked down from heaven and smiled when she saw Samuel training future prophets through his school. Isaiah, Jeremiah and Ezekiel all went to Samuel's school. I know that Hannah was glad she loaned Samuel to the Lord, because her loan is still drawing interest today. That's a high interest rate!

Let your personality be under God's complete control. God wants your personality to draw heavenly interest rates too, and it will when it is totally submitted to Him.

Chapter Eleven

TWO CONFESSIONS FOR A BALANCED PERSONALITY

Your words probably have more to do with the condition of your personality than any other one thing. The Bible tells you so, very plainly, in Proverbs 18:21:

"Death and life are in the power of the tongue: and they that love it shall eat the fruit thereof."

In other words, people who understand the importance of their words are going to be speaking fruitful words with their tongues. Your words, your confessions of faith and of sin, should be the "last word" in maintaining a personality that is balanced by God's Word.

Of course, when I look at the word **confession,** the first thing I think of is the confession of sins. First John 1:9 tells us, *"If we confess our sins, he [God] is faithful and just to forgive us our sins, and to cleanse us from all un-righteousness."* I think it is so great that God not only forgives us, but also He cleanses us! He even wants to clean out the desires that caused us to enter areas of sin. I can think of certain things from my past that are now so far from my personality that I wonder, "How could I ever have done that?" God cleansed me from those things.

The Bible also tells you that, along with the confession of sins, you can confess words to bring life. On one side you see that sin must be confessed in order for you to have a prosperous personality. Proberbs 28:13 tells you that a person who does not confess sin cannot prosper. But on the other hand, if all you did was walk around confessing sin, you would really be a negative person. God said, "Death **and** life are in the power of your tongue." If you only confessed death, would you have life? No! You have to have both, so your second important confession is the confession of **faith.**

What is the confession of faith? It is the confession of God's Word for your life. There is great power in confessing God's Word after you confess sins, and you can see this in the ninth chapter of Nehemiah:

"Now in the twenty and fourth day of this month the children of Israel were assembled with fasting, and with sackclothes, and earth upon them. And the seed of Israel separated themselves from all strangers, and stood and confessed their sins, and the iniquities of their fathers" (Nehemiah 9:1,2).

Notice that the people confessed their fathers' sins in addition to their own sins! Then they followed those confessions with reading the Word of God and confessing His goodness:

"And they stood up in their places, and read in the book of the law of the Lord their God one fourth part of the day; and another fourth part they confessed, and worshipped the Lord their God" (Nehemiah 9:3).

I understand that the "part of the day" spoken of here means a 12-hour period, so it means that for three hours the people read God's Word. Then for the next three hours they confessed the Lord and worshipped Him. Notice that they did these things **after** having confessed their sins. Both confessions must go together to help you maintain a balanced personality. The important thing is that your confession starts with God's Word.

God's Word is as a mirror for both types of confession. The Word first brings repentance because it reveals any areas of sin in your life. After you see the sin, you repent and are cleansed from it. Then God's Word can show you who you are in Christ to build a positive foundation in that area of your personality. That is when your confession of faith comes in and you say, "I always triumph in Christ," or "I am more than a conqueror in Him." Speaking God's Word over your personality reinforces the walls so that they can stand strongly against the enemy, should he attack again.

At the end of Nehemiah chapter nine the Israelites made a covenant with God concerning their lives and personalities. They committed themselves, their actions and their words to God:

> *"Behold, we are servants this day, and for the land that thou gavest unto our fathers to eat the fruit thereof and of the good thereof, behold, we are servants in it: And it yieldeth much increase unto the kings whom thou hast set over us because of our sins: also they have dominion over our bodies, and over our cattle, at their pleasure, and we are in great distress. And because of all this we make a sure covenant, and write it; and our princes, Levites, and priests, seal unto it"* (Nehemiah 9:36-38).

They said, "God, we are confessing our sins. We are also confessing that you are our God who will bring us through, so we make a covenant to keep our confessions right."

The confession of sin and the confession of God's goodness in our lives are so powerful! We need both of them to enhance our relationships with God. The book of Proverbs reveals even more about how your confession affects, not only your personality, but also your health:

"Pleasant words are a honeycomb, sweet to the soul, and health to the bones" (Proverbs 16:24).

When you begin to say good things, you bring health to your soul—which is your mind, your emotions and your will. Do you want a healthy mind and emotional reactions? Do you want a will that constantly chooses God's Word? Then confess the Word of God. It also brings physical health. Do you want a healthy body? Start saying pleasant things, because those words bring life into your physical body.

There is another side to this:

"Heaviness in the heart of a man maketh it stoop: but a good word maketh it glad" (Proverbs 12:25).

If you're walking around saying ugly things about people and circumstances, then the person you hurt the most is yourself. You are going to make your heart stoop, and you are going to make other people's hearts stoop. But you can switch your confession over to the positive and change the situation that was bothering you!

In looking at the life of Elijah, I saw that his confessions consistently took him from one peak of faith to another. His name means "God of salvation," and he was mightily used to show salvation to the nation of Israel during a terrible time of backsliding and sin.

In the book of Deuteronomy God had set forth the conditions of blessings and curses to the children of Israel. He had said, "If you obey My commandments, I will bless you; but if you break My laws, I will close the heavens and make them like iron, and the earth like brass.'' During the days of Elijah Israel found out what God had meant by those scriptures!

Elijah came on the scene as God's prophet after the people of Israel began following a very wicked woman named Jezebel, who led them into idolatry. Her husband's name was Ahab, and he did anything she wanted. He had a spine like a marshmallow! The people fell into idolatry and began to worship Baal, so God told Elijah, "I am closing the heavens, and it will not rain for three-and-a-half years."

"And Elijah the Tishbite, who was of the inhabitants of Gilead, said unto Ahab, As the Lord God of Israel liveth, before whom I stand, there shall not be dew nor rain these years, but according to my word" (1 Kings 17:1).

Ahab had been telling the Israelites, "Your God is dead, and He isn't doing anything for you. You may as well worship Baal." But Elijah said, "The Lord God lives," and proceeded to prophesy of a drought. Then he walked off, leaving Ahab standing there with his mouth hanging open.

After that prophecy God led Elijah to a brook called Cherith, where he would be sustained for a time during the drought. While Elijah stayed at Cherith, the Lord ministered to him, and he drank from the brook. God also used ravens to bring Elijah his food. That seems interesting because, to the Jews, ravens were unclean birds. On top of that, you see that the ravens never ate Elijah's food, even though this was a time of drought. This was God's miracle and plan for Elijah.

After Elijah had stayed at Cherith for many days, the brook began to dry up. God had led Elijah to the brook, so what was wrong? Why would it dry up? When something like this happens, don't just race out and do some big thing on your own. Just hold on, and God will tell you what comes next. Elijah waited, and the Lord spoke to him again:

"Arise, get thee to Zarephath, which belongeth to Zidon, and dwell there: behold, I have commanded a widow there to sustain thee" (1 Kings 17:9).

Zarephath probably wasn't Elijah's favorite place to go, because it was Jezebel's home town. She wasn't living there at the time, but if she decided to visit her mother, aunt, or cousin, she might have run into Elijah. But Elijah didn't seem outwardly nervous. He just obeyed God's voice.

I imagine that Elijah thought the widow who would sustain him was probably loaded with money. He must have been shocked when, after arriving in Zarephath, he encountered a very poor widow who said, "I have only a bit of oil and meal, so I am making a cake for me and my son, and then we will die."

That isn't exactly the kind of widow you would want taking care of you, is it? But she was God's provision for Elijah, and he knew it. He never looked to the widow for help, but instead he just looked to God and helped the widow look to Him also:

"And Elijah said unto her, Fear not; go and do as thou hast said: but make me thereof a little cake first, and bring it to me, and after make for thee and for thy son" (1 Kings 17:13).

The woman barely had enough food for her son and herself! And Elijah wanted some, too? But she had to live by faith, so she baked the man of God his cake and brought it for him. Then Elijah said, *"The barrel of meal shall not waste, neither shall the cruse of oil fail, until the day that the Lord sendeth rain upon the earth"* (1 Kings 17:14).

It is something to stay by a brook, as Elijah did, and be fed by ravens. I think that would take quite a bit of faith! But it is something else to have to believe God, not only for yourself, but also for a widow and her son, too. Elijah was learning the power of confession!

But when you have victories, watch closely, because the enemy wants to steal them from you. After the victory with the oil and meal, the widow's son died, and she really had some deep questions about his death. She told Elijah, *"What have I to do with thee, O thou man of God? art thou come unto me to call my sin to remembrance, and to slay my son?"* (1 Kings 17:18).

Elijah took the woman's son in his arms and carried the body into another room. He prayed, "God, what has happened?" God was leading Elijah step-by-step into a deeper commitment of faith. First he had to believe for his own life. Then he had to believe for two more lives to be sustained. But now he had to believe for the restoration of a life!

He prayed, "Let this child's soul come into him again." God was bringing Elijah into faith for resurrection! The child's soul came into him again, and he lived. The woman was so deeply touched by the miracle that she told Elijah, "I know that thou art a man of God, and that the word of the Lord in thy mouth is truth."

The next step was God preparing Elijah for the biggest moment yet when he was told by God, "Call your people to repentance. For three-and-a-half years it hasn't rained, and it is time for Me to open the heavens again."

Elijah met with Ahab and said, "Call all the prophets of Baal and the people of Israel to Mt. Carmel. Then let's each build an altar with a sacrifice. I will call on the name of the

Lord to consume the sacrifice, and you call on your gods. The god that answers by fire will be God."

Ahab thought that Elijah's suggestion was great, because Baal was supposedly a god of fire. I thought, "You stupid nut, Ahab! Don't you remember that God talked to Moses from a burning bush? Don't you remember that God led the Israelites by fire at night in the wilderness?" You can go through the whole Bible and find that God is a God of fire. Three scripture references in the Bible say that God is a consuming fire! He sent the Holy Ghost and fire, didn't He? Obviously Ahab had no knowledge of the God of Israel.

The Bible didn't give any particular order for the way that Baal's altar was constructed, because it wasn't important. But there is a specific description of how Elijah rebuilt Israel's altar, because God always does things in divine order. I know that the men of Israel came under deep conviction watching the altar being rebuilt. In their days of following Baal the children of Israel had allowed their altar to fall from neglect. It was made from 12 stones, each one representing one of Israel's 12 tribes. Looking on, someone may have said, "That rock stands for my tribe, the tribe of Ahser. I let that rock fall from the altar, but Elijah is restoring it to its rightful place for me."

Elijah told the prophets of Baal, "You call on your gods first, and let's see who answers by fire." The prophets prayed, they screamed, they cut themselves and did all sorts of things. I can't help but laugh at the way Elijah handled the situation—he made fun of them! He said, "Maybe your god is on vacation. Maybe he just can't hear, or is taking a nap, or is deaf."

The sarcastic humor really spurred the false prophets on, but nothing happened. Finally Elijah stopped them and said,

"Enough is enough. Now it's my turn."

Of all things, Elijah brought out 12 barrels of water to pour over the sacrifice. It hadn't rained for over three years, so had we been watching we might have said, "Elijah, what a waste! What are you doing?" But, by faith Elijah was saying, "Each tribe of Israel is going to experience revival!" After pouring the 12 barrels of water on the sacrifice, Elijah prayed this simple prayer:

> *"Hear me, O Lord, hear me, that this people may know that thou art the Lord God, and that thou hast turned their heart back again. Then the fire of the Lord fell, and consumed the burnt sacrifice, and the wood, and the stones, and the dust, and licked up the water that was in the trench" (1 Kings 18:37,38).*

Fire usually doesn't come down, does it? Fire usually goes up! But this was God's fire that consumed the sacrifice, the rubble, the water—everything! God had accepted the sacrifice for the sins of Israel.

> *"And when all the people saw it, they fell on their faces: and they said, The Lord, he is the God; the Lord, he is the God" (1 Kings 18:39).*

Here the people followed the sacrifice for their sin with a confession of God's power. Elijah told them, "Everyone who is for God, stand with me." The Israelites gathered around Elijah and then he said, "Do you see those prophets of Baal? Kill them?" There were hundreds of the false prophets, and all of them were killed that day by the men of Israel.

It was finally time for rain, because the people had repented, had stood up for their God, and had killed the prophets of Baal. There had been repentance from sin, as well as confession of God's goodness.

Elijah sent Ahab away to get some food; Ahab was so carnal! Then Elijah went to the top of the mountain and prayed. "God, we have met the conditions of Your Word, and You said that rain would come." Elijah had a servant with him, whom he told, "Go look toward the sea for any clouds."

The servant looked, came back, and said, "No clouds." But, you see, the Bible tells us to hold fast to our professions of faith without wavering, because God is faithful to His promises. Elijah sent the servant to look for a cloud seven times, and the seventh time the servant said, "I saw a cloud—not a very big one—the size of a man's hand."

Elijah said, "That's it! It is going to rain!" There were no storm clouds, yet Elijah confessed his faith with his mouth. Did he get what he said? Yes, he got it. You will find that through all of Elijah's life, he always confessed things before he saw them. If you see something, you are in the sense realm, not the faith realm. But Elijah was walking in faith, just as we are to walk.

Then Elijah said, "Hurry up, Ahab, let's go before it rains! Ahab started off in a chariot toward his home city, Jezreel, when something wonderful happened to Elijah:

"And the hand of the Lord was on Elijah; and he girded his loins, and ran before Ahab to the entrance of Jezreel" (1 Kings 18:46).

The hands spoken of in this chapter really thrill me. Whenever you confess God's Word, I think you leave your handprint on heaven. I think that when Elijah's servant saw a cloud the size of a man's hand, God was saying, "Elijah, your faith has touched heaven." James 4:8 tells you, *"Draw nigh to God, and he will draw nigh to you."* Whenever you draw close to God with your confession, He also draws close to you. In Elijah's case he was touched by the hand of the Lord, and he ran down the mountain into the next city under an anointing of supernatural strength.

Elijah received what he said. A centurion once told Jesus, "Speak the Word, and my son will be healed." That centurion also received what he said. The little woman who was afflicted with an issue of blood said, "If I may touch the hem of his garment, I shall be whole." She was made whole. Joshua told the sun and the moon to stand still, and they did.

We must watch our confessions. I think that sometimes we need to look in the mirror and say, "God, this mouth has two purposes. It is for confessing sin—my sin, not everybody else's; and it is also for confessing Your Word and its power."

Proverbs 12:14 says, *"A man shall be satisfied with good by the fruit of his mouth."* God wants to satisfy you by the fruit of your mouth! Are you dissatisfied and discontent, yet you don't know why? Perhaps you need to stop speaking words of discontentment.

God wants your thoughts and speech to line up with His Word. Philippians 4:8 is the key:

> *"Finally, brethren, whatsoever things are true, whatsoever things are honest, whatsoever things are just, whatsoever things are pure, whatsoever things are lovely, whatsoever things are of good report; if there be any virtue, and if there be any praise, think on these things."*

You can stabilize your personality totally and overcome the enemy by being established in these two confessions: the confession of sin and the confession of faith. Psalm 17:4 says, *"Concerning the works of men, by the word of thy lips I have kept me from the destroyer."*

125

The enemy would come in and pull down the walls and gates of your personality. But you overcame the enemy to your personality through diligence in your confession. Give your personality a good report with the Word, and you will accelerate the Lord's work in conforming your personality to that of His Son. Remember, it is God who works in you, to will and to do his good pleasure.

Chapter Twelve

OUR PERSONALITIES ARE IMPORTANT TO GOD

HIS VISION FOR YOU

Have you ever felt as though you were just one in a crowd and God wasn't personally concerned about you? I think that all of us have felt like this, especially at times when the enemy was trying to get us into a negative frame of mind. Maybe these thoughts came when negative circumstances seemed overwhelming, or when we didn't feel good physically. Sometimes we feel this way when, after having prayed about something for years, we just get upset with the Lord and say, "What do You care?"

I want you to know that God **is** personally concerned about you, and you are not lost in a crowd. You can see this by looking at a woman who appeared to have been lost in a crowd, but she wasn't lost to Jesus. To God, we aren't lost at all. In fact, there could be a crowd of one-million people, and if one of them had faith, God would see it. He sees faith and is attracted by faith.

The woman in the crowd had an issue of blood, and her story is told in three of the four gospels. History tells you that she was a gentile from Cesarea, but all I know is that she was considered to be "unclean."

The woman had done every possible thing to obtain a cure, had spent every penny she owned, yet the issue of blood remained. As her story unfolds, you find that she was confessing something with her mouth, however, that radically changed her personality, spirit, and physical body as no earthly physician could!

The woman heard that Jesus was passing through the streets of her town, and she heard that He had done many miracles for people. She thought, "I've got to get in on this."

The woman rushed out to the street where Jesus was, and she probably fought her way past hundreds of people who were following Him that day. Then she did something unusual. She did not come up and touch his shoulder or arm. She did not confront the Lord and ask Him for healing. Instead, she bent forward and reached out to touch the hem of the Lord's garment.

Why didn't the woman just come up right in front of Jesus? She couldn't do that because, by Levitical law, her unclean state prevented her from touching any man while she had an issue of blood. Anything she touched or sat upon had to be cleansed in a special way. Not only was the woman physically miserable, but her social and spiritual life suffered, too. She was cut off from worship because an unclean person could not enter the synagogue. She couldn't go anywhere with friends because she couldn't touch things. She had tried everything, and Jesus was her last resort. How many times do we make Jesus our last resort? But last or not, He gave the woman what she needed. The scriptural accounts tell of the woman's healing in several different ways:

"And a woman having an issue of blood twelve years, which had spent all her living upon physicians, neither could be healed of any, Came behind him [Jesus], and touched the border of this garment: and immediately her issue of blood stanched" (Luke 8:43,44).

"For she said, If I may touch but his clothes, I shall be whole. And straightway the fountain of her blood was dried up; and she felt in her body that she was healed of that plaque" (Mark 5:28,29).

I thought it was interesting that the fountain of blood, the source of the woman's issue of blood, was healed. Sometimes symptoms are taken care of through medication, but we don't cure the actual sickness. For instance, we may take something to ease the headache and sneezing of a cold, but not actually be rid of the cold itself. But this woman knew in herself that she had been completely healed of the plague that she had suffered.

When the woman touched the hem of Jesus' garment, He stopped in His tracks, looked around and said, "Who touched Me?"

Peter said, "That isn't a very sensible question. Here we are in a crowd of people where everyone is touching You, and you ask, 'Who touched Me?' Everyone is touching You!"

Then Jesus said, "Somebody touched me because I can tell that virtue has gone out of my body." The word **virtue** does not mean "moral excellence," as we today think of **virtue**. Of course, Jesus **was** morally excellent, but in this passage of text the Greek word for **virtue** is **dunamis,** or "miracle-working power." Jesus was saying, "Somebody touched me in faith, and it drew miracle power from My being."

You can't ever touch Jesus in faith without receiving the miracle power you need for your situation. The woman knew that she had no choice but to confess what had happened when the Lord asked, "Who touched Me?" She knew that, according to the Levitical law, she had been wrong to touch Jesus. Trembling, she stepped up in front of Him and declared before Him and all the people why she had touched Him and that she had been healed immediately.

I believe that Jesus called the woman apart from the crowd because He wanted her to confess her faith. In Matthew 10:32 Jesus said, *"Whosoever therefore shall confess me before men, him will I confess also before my Father which is in heaven."* When the woman confessed her faith in front of the crowd, Jesus spoke tenderly, *"Daughter, be of good comfort; thy faith hath made thee whole; go in peace"* (Luke 8:48).

When the woman confessed her faith in the Lord, she received far more than healing. She was an outcast, a gentile who had been unclean, yet Jesus called her "Daughter." Then He said, "Be of good comfort," and the word **comfort** is a really great word. It means "strength." If you had an issue of blood for 12 years, you would be in a very weak condition. How could you help but be weak, no matter how good your nutritional intake was? But Jesus gave the woman strength and I believe that she received back all the strength she had lost during her 12 years of sickness.

Then the Lord told the woman, "Your faith has made you whole." Notice that He didn't say, "**My** faith has made you whole." The word **whole** means "complete," as we think of it, but it also means "saved from sin." The word **holy** means "complete," so now the woman had been made holy. A person who is not a Christian may have a healthy physical body and sound mental health, but he is still incomplete in his spirit; he is not holy. But this woman was made complete in her body, her personality and her spirit.

Not only did Jesus save the woman, give her strength, and call her "Daughter," for her confession of faith, but He also said, "Go in peace." She had taken a risk in standing before hundreds of people to tell the Lord what she had done. Now she could go in a spirit of peace.

After reading the story of this woman's healing, I could not help but wonder why she reached down to touch the hem of the Lord's garment. Why not brush by his shoulder? Wouldn't that be as effective? I found my answer in Numbers 15:

> *"And the Lord spake unto Moses, saying, Speak unto the children of Israel, and bid them that they make them fringes in the borders of their garments throughout their generations, and that they put upon the fringe of the borders a ribband of blue: And it shall be unto you for a fringe, that ye may look upon it, and remember all the commandments of the Lord, and do them" (Numbers 15:37-39a).*

God said, "I want all of the sons of Israel to have a fringe on their garments to remind them of My commandments. This fringe will remind them of My presence." By seeing the fringes on their garments, the men of Israel would be reminded that God was their Lord, and they were not to be involved with idols.

Blue has always signified divinity, so the ribbon of blue underneath the fringe represented the presence of God. That little ribbon of blue was saying, "Wherever I go, the presence of God goes with me. I want to go God's way."

The woman with the issue of blood had reached through the crowd to touch the presence of God! Even though she had been just one in a crowd, her faith had set her apart. When Jesus called her before Him, she was face-to-face with the Son of God. I'm sure that, to her, it didn't appear that there was anyone else present except just her and Jesus. God loves every one of us just as though there were only one to love.

I especially like the account of the woman's healing in Matthew, which tells us that when the woman heard about Jesus, she *"said within herself, If I may but touch his garment, I shall be whole" (9:21)*. The woman received **exactly** what she said: wholeness in her spirit, soul and body. Apparently there were 11 reported cures for an issue of blood, but none of them had worked. Yet because of her words, the source of her issue of blood dried up when she touched the Lord's garment. Then Jesus did not say, "My faith healed you." He said, "Your faith healed you." Phileomon 6 tells you how faith is released:

> *"That the communication of thy faith may become effectual by the acknowledging of every good thing which is in you in Christ Jesus" (Philemon 6).*

How do you turn your faith loose? The woman made her faith effectual, or "energetic," by speaking it with her mouth: "If I touch the hem of his garment I shall be whole." Why? Because she knew that she was touching the presence and anointing of God.

There is a beautiful psalm about a priest and his anointing. It is Psalm 133:2 that says of the anointing, *"It is like the precious ointment upon the head, that ran down upon the beard, even Aaron's beard: that went down to the skirts of his garments."* The anointing of Aaron to priesthood started at the top of his head and flowed down past the skirts of his garment to his feet. Aaron was a high priest, but Jesus is **the** High Priest, whose garment you can touch by faith today.

Do you need an anointing of healing in your personality? Perhaps you have struggled with a bad temper. Maybe you have just been living in defeat. Whatever the problem, Jesus wants to change your life through the words you speak. By speaking words of faith, you are reaching out and touching the presence of God. You aren't "just another person in the crowd. Your faith will set you apart. That's the key to your entire personality transformation: turn your faith loose! You turn your faith loose by turning your mouth loose—and by doing so you loose wholeness for your personality.

HIS VISIONS FOR OTHERS

Since God is personally concerned about our individual personalities, it is important that we, in turn, are concerned with the personalities of others. God doesn't save us so that we can sit around and do nothing. He saves us so that we can share what we have with the rest of the world.

In the New Testament a man named Barnabas gave us a beautiful example of how we can, by faith, get God's vision of transformation for others as well as ourselves. Barnabas was a New Testament prophet whose name means "son of consolation." Barnabas was a Levite from the little island of Cyprus. Evidently he was very wealthy, for the Bible speaks of how he came to the apostles and laid all of his possessions at their feet in his commitment to the ministry. He was very excited about the gospel and the idea of seeing the Body of Christ brought to completion.

One day Barnabas heard about a man who was preaching the gospel. Everyone was afraid to talk to the man because, in the past, he had been guilty of persecuting and killing many Christians. In fact, he had consented to the death of Stephen, one of the church's primary deacons. The disciples of Jesus thought, "This is a trap. He wants to get our names so that he can have us killed."

Barnabas decided to check out the situation. When he heard Paul preach, he knew without reservation that the man had definitely met the living Christ:

> *"But Barnabas took him, and brought him to the apostles, and declared unto them how he had seen the Lord in the way, and that he had spoken to him, and how he had preached boldly at Damascus in the name of Jesus" (Acts 9:27).*

The man whom Barnabas brought to the apostles had been named Saul. He was a devoted Pharisee who had studied the scripture at the feet of Gamaliel, one of the day's most learned Jews. Saul would become Paul, the apostle who would write more than half of the New Testament—a paradox to both Jews and Christians alike. Who brought him to the apostles for acceptance? It was Barnabas.

Barnabas was concerned that the Body of Christ obtain the fullest benefit from its new converts. He wasn't content with just seeing people converted, but was interested in people's spiritual growth afterward. Whenever you read about Barnabas, he was making good confessions about others. It's one thing to make a good confession for yourself: the woman with the issue of blood confessed that the Lord could make her whole. But we can get so hung up on ourselves that we forget how God wants to use us in the personalities of other people. We need to make good confessions for them, too.

The next positive confession made by Barnabas is found in Acts chapter 11. A tremendous revival broke out among the gentiles, and Barnabas' first reaction was, "These people need to hear from Saul!"

"Then departed Barnabas for Tarsus, for to seek Saul: And when he had found him, he brought him unto Antioch. And it came to pass, that a whole year they assembled themselves with the church, and taught much people. And the disciples were called Christians first in Antioch" (Acts 11:25-27).

Barnabas thought, "Saul has been educated by the best teachers, so he fully understands the meaning of the New Testament. He knows the Word well, and he has had personal experience with Jesus Christ." When Barnabas brought Saul to the gentiles as a teacher, you see that while Saul was teaching, God used the time as a training period before the full-time ministry abroad.

God uses everything possible in your life to prepare you for your next step. God's divine goal for Christians is that they be conformed to the image of Christ Jesus. But there is also a plan for your individual life. And God wants to prepare you to fulfill that plan. He definitely used Saul's time in Antioch as preparation for what would be the first missionary journey.

Eventually Barnabas and Saul took a young, on-fire convert named John Mark under their wing, to train him in the ministry. Shortly afterward Barnabas and Saul were set apart for their ministries of evangelism:

"As they ministered to the Lord, and fasted, the Holy Ghost said, Separate me Barnabas and Saul for the work whereunto I have called them. And when they had fasted and prayed, and laid their hands on them, they sent them away" (Acts 13:2,3).

Those ministering and fasting with Saul and Barnabas laid

hands on them and sent them forth to preach. From that time on, Saul's name was changed to Paul. Nothing in the scriptures is an accident, of course, so why the name change? Later on you see that Paul had a very definite call to preach to the gentiles. His Jewish name had been Saul, but now he needed a gentile name: **Paul.**

Paul and Barnabas started out on their journey, and they brought John Mark with them. Some really tremendous things happened, but one of the low points of the mission was when John Mark became very homesick and had to return to Antioch. Apparently this really disgusted Paul. Nonetheless, there were many miracles on this first missionary journey.

When Barnabas and Paul returned to Antioch, the people were thrilled to hear about the wonderful things that had happened to the men. Not long afterward they decided to return to the cities where men had received the Lord. Barnabas told Paul, "Let's give John Mark a second chance."

Paul said, "No, I wouldn't think of taking him. He's just a mama's boy. He had to go home before we completed the first missionary journey, and he'll probably do it again."

I love what Acts 15:37 says: *"And Barnabas determined to take with them John, whose surname was Mark."* Barnabas was determined that this young convert's ministry would be developed. His confession about other personalities is so positive!

Barnabas' insistence that John Mark go on the mission just made Paul more angry, and there were very sharp words between him and Barnabas. Finally they agreed to go on separate journeys: Paul would go with Silas, and Barnabas would take John Mark.

It seems such a shame that Paul and Barnabas had a disagreement, but the story still has a happy ending. Mark, under Barnabas' instruction, began to develop in ministry. He may have been a baby on the first journey, but he grew up.

After the missionary journey Mark became such an ardent follower of Jesus that the apostle Peter became his tutor. Peter loved Mark so much that later Peter called him "My son." Mark, being like Peter's son, heard the instructor's every word about Jesus. Mark soaked in one firsthand account after another. Then God began to speak to Mark about writing a gospel.

Mark could have said, "I'm not worthy. I was never an original apostle." But God said, "You were taught by an original apostle, and I want you to write his words down."

Today the gospel of Mark that you read was written by the Mark about whom Paul said, "No way. He'll never amount to anything." Mark might have just given up on the ministry because he had been turned down by those more seasoned in the ministry than he was. But Barnabas saw beyond appearances and received a vision of faith for the young man.

This story ends so beautifully with Mark ultimately accepted by Paul. To the Colossians Paul wrote, "Be sure and receive Mark," and then in 2 Timothy 4:11 Paul said, "Bring me Mark because he is profitable for the ministry." What a compliment to Mark! Not only did Paul say, "He is a good minister," but also, "I need him here." Mark, the deserter, became Mark, the minister and writer of the gospel.

Did Barnabas and Paul ever make up? Yes, because Paul wrote about Barnabas in 1 Corinthians 9, which was written after the book of Acts. Maybe Paul told Barnabas, "I'm going to have to learn to like meat, because I have to eat crow. I never thought that Mark would work out, and you showed me differently. Your positive confession made him profitable in the ministry.''

I want you to know that God has sent you to have more than just a personality change in your own life. He wants you to help others have changes of personality in their lives. God wants you ministering to others with honest words of faith. He wants you to use positive words to build character.

How did Barnabas know that ''Saul'' would become ''Paul'' and that Mark would become a mighty minister of Christ? He knew because he looked beyond God's concern for his own personality and loved others deeply enough to extend that same concern to them. After all, the beauty in a personality that is complete in Jesus Christ is that it reaches out to help transform the personalities of others.

Receive Jesus Christ as Lord and Savior of Your Life.

The Bible says, *"That if thou shalt confess with thy mouth the Lord Jesus, and shalt believe in thine heart that God hath raised him from the dead, thou shalt be saved. For with the heart man believeth unto righteousness; and with the mouth confession is made unto salvation"* (Romans 10:9,10).

To receive Jesus Christ as Lord and Savior of your life, sincerely pray this prayer from your heart:

Dear Jesus,

I believe that You died for me and that You rose again on the third day. I confess to You that I am a sinner and that I need Your love and forgiveness. Come into my life, forgive my sins, and give me eternal life. I confess You now as my Lord. Thank You for my salvation!

Signed _____

Date _____

Write to us.

We will send you information to help you with your new life in Christ.

Marilyn Hickey Ministries • P.O. Box 17340
Denver, CO 80217 • (303) 770-0400

Prayer Request(s)

Let us join our faith with yours for your prayer needs. Fill out the coupon below and send to Marilyn Hickey Ministries, P.O. Box 17340, Denver, CO 80217.

Prayer Request(s) _____

_____

_____

_____

_____

_____

Mr. & Mrs.   Please print.
Mr.
Name Miss _____
     Mrs.

Address _____

City _____

State _____ Zip _____

Phone(H) (   ) _____

(W) (   ) _____

If you want prayer immediately, call our Prayer Center at (303) 796-1333, Monday-Friday, 4 a.m. - 4:30 p.m. (MT).

For Your Information
Free Monthly Magazine

☐ Please send me your free monthly magazine OUTPOURING (including daily devotionals, timely articles, and ministry updates)!

Tapes and Books

☐ Please send me Marilyn's latest product catalog.

Mr. & Mrs.
Miss
Mrs.   Please print.
Name Mr. _____

Address _____

City _____

State _____ Zip _____

Phone (H) ( ) _____

(W) ( ) _____

Mail to
Marilyn Hickey Ministries
P.O. Box 17340
Denver, CO 80217
(303) 770-0400

BOOKS BY MARILYN HICKEY

A Cry for Miracles ($7.95)
Acts of the Holy Spirit ($7.95)
Angels All Around ($7.95)
Armageddon ($4.95)
Ask Marilyn ($9.95)
Be Healed ($9.95)
Blessing Journal ($4.95)
Bible Encounter Classic Edition
  ($24.95)
Book of Revelation Comic Book
  (The) ($3.00)
Break the Generation Curse
  ($7.95)
Break the Generation Curse
  Part 2 ($9.95)
Building Blocks for Better Families
  ($4.95)
Daily Devotional ($7.95)
Dear Marilyn ($7.95)
Devils, Demons, and Deliverance
  ($9.95)
Divorce Is Not the Answer ($7.95)
Especially for Today's Woman
  ($14.95)
Freedom From Bondages ($7.95)
Gift-Wrapped Fruit ($2.95)
God's Covenant for Your Family
  ($7.95)

God's Rx for a Hurting Heart ($4.95)
Hebrew Honey ($14.95)
How to Be a Mature Christian ($7.95)
Know Your Ministry ($4.95)
Maximize Your Day . . . God's Way
  ($7.95)
Miracle Signs and Wonders ($24.95)
Names of God (The) ($7.95)
Nehemiah—Rebuilding the Broken
  Places in Your Life ($7.95)
No. 1 Key to Success—Meditation
  (The) ($4.95)
Proverbs Classic Library Edition
  ($24.95)
Release the Power of the Blood
  Covenant ($4.95)
Satan-Proof Your Home ($7.95)
Save the Family Promise Book
  ($14.95)
Signs in the Heavens ($7.95)
What Every Person Wants to Know
  About Prayer ($4.95)
When Only a Miracle Will Do ($4.95)
Your Miracle Source ($4.95)
Your Total Health Handbook—Body
  • Soul • Spirit ($9.95)

MINI-BOOKS: $1⁰⁰ each
by Marilyn Hickey

Beat Tension
Bold Men Win
Bulldog Faith
Change Your Life
Children Who Hit the Mark
Conquering Setbacks
Don't Park Here
Experience Long Life
Fasting and Prayer
God's Benefit: Healing
God's Seven Keys to Make You Rich
Hold On to Your Dream
How to Become More Than a
  Conqueror
How to Win Friends
I Can Be Born Again and Spirit Filled

I Can Dare to Be an Achiever
Keys to Healing Rejection
Power of Forgiveness (The)
Power of the Blood (The)
Receiving Resurrection Power
Renew Your Mind
Solving Life's Problems
Speak the Word
Standing in the Gap
Story of Esther (The)
Tithes • Offerings • Alms • God's
  Plan for Blessing You
Turning Point
Winning Over Weight
Women of the Word

Prices are in U.S. dollars. If ordering in foreign currency, please calculate the current exchange rate.

Marilyn Hickey Ministries

Marilyn was a public school teacher when she met Wallace Hickey. After their marriage, Wally was called to the ministry and Marilyn began teaching home Bible studies.

The vision of Marilyn Hickey Ministries is to "cover the earth with the Word" (Isaiah 11:9). For over 30 years Marilyn Hickey has dedicated herself to an anointed, unique, and distinguished ministry of reaching out to people—from all walks of life—who are hungry for God's Word and all that He has for them. Millions have witnessed and acclaimed the positive, personal impact she brings through fresh revelation knowledge that God has given her through His Word.

Marilyn has been the invited guest of government leaders and heads of state from many nations of the world. She is considered by many to be one of today's greatest ambassadors of God's Good News to this dark and hurting generation.

The more Marilyn follows God's will for her life, the more God uses her to bring refreshing, renewal, and revival to the Body of Christ throughout the world. As His obedient servant, Marilyn desires to follow Him all the days of her life.

Marilyn and Wally adopted their son Michael; through a fulfilled prophecy they had their daughter Sarah, who with her husband Reece, is now part of the ministry.

Marilyn founded her ministry "Life for Laymen" so that she could reach more people with her gift for practical Bible application.

Marilyn taught at Denver's "Happy Church" and hosted ministry conferences with husband Wally.

At a retreat in 1976, Marilyn realized she was called to "cover the earth with the Word."

The ministry staff in the early days helped Marilyn answer the mail that came in response to her first 15-minute radio show.

Soon Marilyn realized how many more people she could reach by going on television. She and Wally hosted many well known guests.

In Guatemala with former President Ephraim Rios-Mott

Marilyn has been the invited guest of government leaders and heads of state from many nations of the world.

In Egypt with Mrs. Anwar Sadat

In Venezuela with first lady Mrs. Perez

In Lebanon with Major Haddad

Marilyn ministers to guerillas in Honduras and brings food and clothing to the wives and children who are encamped with their husbands.

The popular Bible reading plan "Time With Him" began in 1978 and invited people to "read through the Bible with Marilyn." The monthly ministry magazine has since been renamed "Outpouring." It now includes a calendar of ministry events, timely articles, and featured product offers.

Through Word to the World College (formerly Marilyn Hickey Bible College), Marilyn is helping to equip men and women to take the gospel around the world.

Recently dorms were added to the campus facilities.

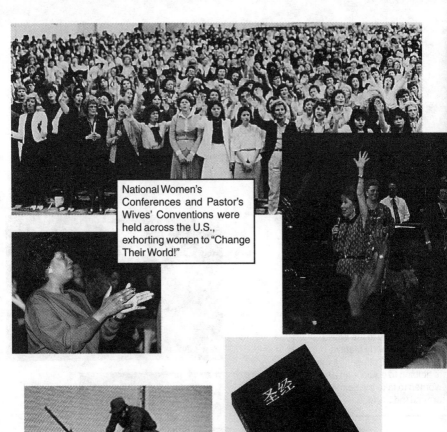

National Women's Conferences and Pastor's Wives' Conventions were held across the U.S., exhorting women to "Change Their World!"

God began to open doors for the supplying of Bibles to many foreign lands—China, Israel, Poland, Ethiopia, Russia, Romania, and Ukraine, just to name a few.

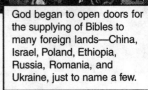

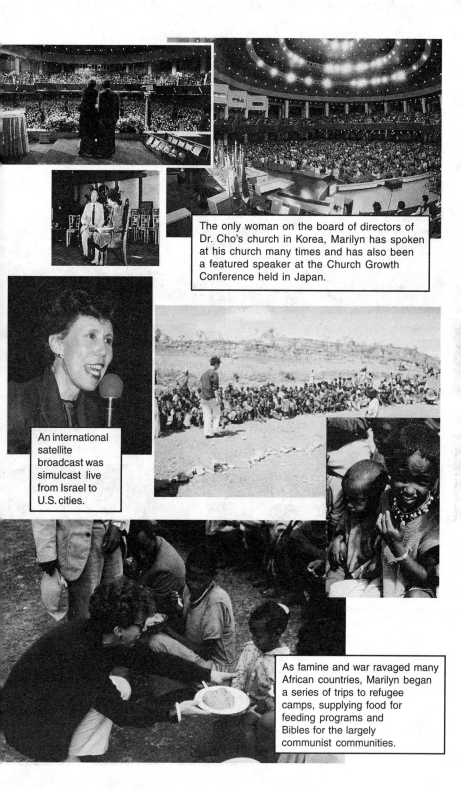

The only woman on the board of directors of Dr. Cho's church in Korea, Marilyn has spoken at his church many times and has also been a featured speaker at the Church Growth Conference held in Japan.

An international satellite broadcast was simulcast live from Israel to U.S. cities.

As famine and war ravaged many African countries, Marilyn began a series of trips to refugee camps, supplying food for feeding programs and Bibles for the largely communist communities.

The ministry expanded from its beginnings in a cardboard box, to the first International Ministry Center, built in 1985, to present headquarters located in Greenwood Village, Colorado.

FILL THE SHIP, a special project of the Marilyn Hickey Children's Fund, supplies food and Bibles to various Third World countries, such as Haiti, the Philippines, Ethiopia, Honduras, and El Salvador.

The prime time television special, "A Cry for Miracles," featured co-host Gavin MacLeod.

Over 1,500 ministry products help people in all areas of their life.

Marilyn Hickey's Prayer Center handles calls from all over the U.S.— ministering to those who need agreement in prayer.

Marilyn ministered in underground churches in Romania before any of the European communist countries were officially open.

Ministry and speaking engagement at a Women's Conference in Nigeria

Marilyn receives her honorary doctorate from Oral Roberts University.

Marilyn and her Faith Covenant Partners respond to countless needs across the world ... the devastating earthquakes in Mexico City, Romanian orphans, leprosy victims in Africa, orphans in war torn Rwanda, street children in Brazil, ... all are touched by God's power.

Marilyn has been a guest several times on the 700 Club with host Pat Robertson.

Airlift Manila provided much needed food, Bibles, and personal supplies to the Philippines; MHM also raised funds to aid in the digging of water wells for those without clean drinking water.

Marilyn participates in a "devil-stomp" on prayer requests: thousands are received daily from friends and partners all over the world and are prayed over by Marilyn and the staff.

MHM supports Mission of Mercy in Calcutta, headed by Huldah Buntain. Marilyn has made several trips there.

Missions' trips to China are really close to Marilyn's and Sarah's hearts. Thousands of Bibles have been smuggled across the borders.

"Today With Marilyn" Bible teaching program is broadcast weekdays on TBN, BET, and several independent stations. The program is also seen overseas by millions through Rhema Network South Africa, in Australia on Network 10, and in more than 80 other countries worldwide.

Marilyn ministers to and teaches thousands at Encounters and Miracle Healing Crusades overseas, as well as in the U.S.

Exciting ministry opportunities awaited Marilyn and her team of travelers in Ukraine and Russia, as the doors opened for the Gospel.

Victim of the nuclear power plant disaster in Chernobyl

Marilyn has held Bible Encounters in Malaysia and Singapore. While traveling through Hong Kong she ministered to Vietnamese in a refugee camp.

Ministry trips and cruises to places such as Indonesia, Russia, Greece, Ukraine, Turkey, and Israel offer short-term missions' opportunities to travel with Marilyn to exotic places.

Overseas offices have recently been set up in the United Kingdom, Australia, and South Africa. Marilyn also hosts yearly meetings, crusades, and missions' projects in those countries.

Crowds of up to 200,000 attended the open-air crusade in Bangalore, India.

In Islamabad, Pakistan, Marilyn held Ministry Training Schools. Total crusade attendance was estimated at 70,000.

Eritrea and Sudan—Ministry Training Schools, nightly crusades and Madagascar crusade with Sarah and Marilyn ministering